Writing Program Administration
Journal of the
Council of Writing Program Administrators

Guest Editorial Coordinators
Lisa Mastrangelo .... Centenary University
Mark Blaauw-Hara .... University of Toronto Mississauga

Guest Copy Editors
Doug Hesse ....University of Denver
Joe Janangelo ....Loyola University Chicago
Susan Miller-Cochran..University of Arizona
Duane Roen.. Arizona State University
Shirley Rose .... Arizona State University
Kathleen Blake Yancey... Florida State University

Editorial Board
Nancy Bou Ayash .... University of Washington
David Blakesley .... Clemson University
Beth Brunk-Chavez..University of Texas at El Paso
Sheila Carter-Tod ....Virginia Tech
Chen Chen ....Winthrop University
Sherri Craig .... West Chester University
Casie Fedukovich .... North Carolina State University
Carolyn (Collie) Fulford ....North Carolina Central University
David Green .... Howard University
Teresa Grettano .... University of Scranton
Sarah Z. Johnson ....Madison College
Alexandria Lockett ....Spelman College
Staci Perryman-Clark .... Western Michigan University
Patti Poblete... Henderson State University
Amy Ferdinandt Stolley ....Grand Valley State University
Darci Thoune... University of Wisconsin–LaCrosse
Peter Vandenberg ....DePaul University

Production and distribution of *WPA: Writing Program Administration* is managed by Parlor Press.

Council of Writing Program Administrators

Executive Board

Susan Thomas, President .... University of Sydney
Lilian Mina, Vice President .... Auburn University at Montgomery
Mark Blaauw-Hara, Past President .... University of Toronto Mississauga
Patti Poblete .... Henderson State University
Melvin Beavers .... University of Arkansas at Little Rock
Al Harahap .... University of Oklahoma
Erin Lehman .... Ivy Tech Community College of Indiana
Annie Del Principe .... Kingsborough Community College
Derek Mueller .... Virginia Tech
Katherine Daily O'Meara .... St. Norbert College
Sarah Snyder .... Arizona Western College
Julia Voss .... Santa Clara University

Ex Officio Members

Sherry Rankins-Robertson, Treasurer .... University of Central Florida
Kelley Blewett, Secretary .... Indana University East
Shirley K Rose, Co-Director CES .... Arizona State University
Michael Pemberton, Co-Director, CES .... Georgia Southern University

Guide for Authors

WPA: Writing Program Administration publishes empirical and theoretical research on issues in writing program administration. We publish a wide range of research in various formats, research that not only helps both titled and untitled administrators of writing programs do their jobs, but also helps our discipline advance academically, institutionally, and nationally.
Possible topics of interest include:

- writing faculty professional development
- writing program creation and design
- uses for national learning outcomes and statements that impact writing programs
- classroom research studies
- labor conditions: material, practical, fiscal
- WAC/WID/WC/CAC (or other sites of communication/writing in academic settings)
- writing centers and writing center studies
- teaching writing with electronic texts (multimodality) and teaching in digital spaces
- theory, practice, and philosophy of writing program administration
- outreach and advocacy
- curriculum development
- writing program assessment
- WPA history and historical work
- national and regional trends in education and their impact on WPA work
- issues of professional advancement and writing program administration
- diversity and WPA work
- writing programs in a variety of educational locations (SLACs, HBCUs, two-year colleges, Hispanic schools, non-traditional schools, dual credit or concurrent enrollment programs, prison writing programs)
- interdisciplinary work that informs WPA practices

This list is meant to be suggestive, not exhaustive. Contributions must be appropriate to the interests and concerns of the journal and its readership. The editors welcome empirical research (quantitative as well as qualitative), historical research, and theoretical, essayistic, and practical pieces.

Submission Guidelines

Please check the *WPA* website for complete submissions guidelines and to download the required coversheet. In general, submissions should:

- be a maximum 7,500 words;
- be styled according to either the *MLA Handbook* (8th edition) or the *Publication Manual of the American Psychological Association* (7th edition), as appropriate to the nature of your research;

- include an abstract (maximum 200 words);
- contain no identifying information;
- be submitted as a .doc or .docx format file; and
- use tables, notes, figures, and appendices sparingly and judiciously.

Submissions that do not follow these guidelines or that are missing the cover page will be returned to authors before review.

Reviews

WPA:Writing Program Administration publishes both review essays of multiple books and reviews of individual books related to writing programs and their administration. If you are interested in reviewing texts or recommending books for possible review, please contact the book review editor at wpabookreviews@gmail.com.

Announcements and Calls

Relevant announcements and calls for papers may be published as space permits. Announcements should not exceed 500 words, and calls for proposals or participation should not exceed 1,000 words. Submission deadlines in calls should be no sooner than January 1 for the fall issue and June 1 for the spring issue. Please email your calls and announcements to wpaeditors@gmail.com and include the text in both the body of the message and as a .doc or .docx attachment.

Correspondence

Correspondence relating to the journal, submissions, or editorial issues should be sent to wpaeditors@gmail.com.

Subscriptions

WPA: Writing Program Administration is published twice per year—fall and spring—by the Council of Writing Program Administrators. Members of the council receive a subscription to the journal and access to the *WPA* archives as part of their membership. Join the council at http://wpacouncil.org. Information about library subscriptions is available at http://wpacouncil.org/aws/CWPA/pt/sp/journal-subscriptions.

Writing Program Administration

Journal of the
Council of Writing Program Administrators
Volume 45.1 (Fall 2021)

Contents

Letter from the Editorial Coordinators 7

Essays

In the Event of an Emergency: Crisis Management for WPAs 9
  Kaitlin Clinnin

Vision and Visibility: A Call to Feminist WPAs 31
  Casie Fedukovich

Dedicating Time and Space for Women to Succeed
in the Academy: A Case Analysis of a Women Faculty
Writing Program at a Research 1 Institution 50
  Kristin Messuri and Elizabeth A. Sharp

How Can We Better Support Teaching Multimodal Composition?
A National Survey of Institutional Professional
Development Efforts 70
  Chen Chen

The Tacit Values of Sourced Writing: A Study of
Source "Engagement" and the FYW Program as
Community of Practice 91
  Donna Scheidt and Holly Middleton

"I Know It's Going to Affect My Teaching": What Emerging
Teachers Learn through Tutoring Writing 110
  Dorothy Worden-Chambers and Amy E. Dayton

**The Laborious Reality vs. the Imagined Ideal of
Graduate Student Instructors of Writing**... 131
    Ruth Osorio, Allison Hutchison, Sarah Primeau, Molly E.
    Ubbesen, and Alexander Champoux-Crowley

Book Review

**Emotional Identity and Dexterity: A Review of
*The Things We Carry***... 152
    Jackie Hoermann-Elliott

Review Essay

**Compassion and Social Justice: What We Can Learn from
*Sixteen Teachers Teaching*** 158
    Charles Grimm

Letter from the Editorial Coordinators

Stepping into editing an issue of a journal is much like stepping into someone else's class after the semester has already started. Yes, you've done this before, and you know that you *should* know where the dry-erase markers are and how to fire up the whiteboard, but it's decidedly awkward and produces even more jitters than the first day of the semester. The outgoing editorial crew of Lori Ostergaard, Jim Nugent, Jacob Babb, Courtney Adams Wooten, and their entire team had set the bar high during their tenure, and the summer special issue that focused on racial justice—guest edited by Sheila Carter-Tod and Jennifer Sano-Franchini—raised that bar even higher.

Luckily, we had an impressive group of authors with which to work, and the outgoing editors had already worked with them to fine-tune their already excellent manuscripts. These authors responded quickly and thoughtfully to our (many) requests for information and clarifications. Their willingness to be responsive to us made our jobs all the easier.

To add to our good fortune, an amazing team of CWPA Past Presidents agreed to serve in editorial positions. While we managed the technical end of things, these Past Presidents did the actual work of copy-editing manuscripts, which requires careful attention and involves looking up subject-verb agreements you absolutely swore you already knew—not to mention recently updated citation formats. But Shirley Rose, Susan Miller-Cochran, Doug Hesse, Joe Janangelo, Duane Roen, and Kathleen Blake Yancey stepped in with grace, good humor, and a gift for language, for which we are extremely grateful. Together, we were able to put together an issue of *WPA: Writing Program Administration* that features the great writing and excellent scholarship that has been the hallmark of the journal.

And yes, let's talk about you. We'd like to thank you for reading this journal. Without readers, a journal is just an exercise—one doomed to irrelevancy. Yet you have stuck by *WPA* and helped it grow into a defining journal in our field. We are grateful for that.

In this issue, you'll find an essay by Kaitlin Clinnin outlining an approach to writing-program crisis management. Casie Fedukovich then explores feminist leadership, and Kristin Messuri and Elizabeth A. Sharp write about a women-faculty writing program. Chen Chen suggests professional-development interventions to support the teaching of multimodal writing. Donna Scheidt and Holly Middleton explore how a FYW program is a community of practice. Dorothy Worden-Chambers and Amy E. Dayton detail a study of writing-center tutors with an eye to what they learned about teaching. And Ruth Osorio, Allison Hutchison, Sarah Primeau, Molly E. Ubbesen, and Alexander Champoux-Crowle present the conclusions from a large-scale survey of graduate-student writing instructors that sheds light on material challenges and labor inequities. This issue also includes two excellent review essays: Jackie Hoermann-Elliott's review of Courtney Adams Wooten, Jacob Babb, Kristi Murray Costello, and Kate Navickas's book *The Things We Carry*, and Charles Grimm's review of Patrick Sullivan's *Sixteen Teachers Teaching*.

So yes—we did the equivalent of stumbling around trying to find the dry-erase markers and calling tech support to turn on the projector. We asked our wonderful publisher, David Blakesley, and the outgoing editors so many questions that we can never repay them, and we are so grateful for their help. But in the end, we are so pleased with the result, and we think you will be as well.

Warmly,

Lisa Mastrangelo and Mark Blaauw-Hara
Co-Editorial Coordinators

Essays

In the Event of an Emergency: Crisis Management for WPAs

Kaitlin Clinnin

ABSTRACT

In this article, I argue that WPAs must proactively engage in a crisis management process to create crisis-ready writing programs. Crises disrupt the typical writing program work, so WPAs must be prepared to collaborate with existing campus-crisis response plans and develop their own programmatic crisis management plans. Drawing on my experience as a WPA after an off-campus mass shooting and a global pandemic, I present a process that WPAs can use to prevent, prepare for, respond to, and recover from crisis events. This crisis management process will help WPAs create writing programs that are more attentive to writing program stakeholders' changing educational and socio-emotional needs after a crisis so that the work of teaching and learning about writing can resume as quickly and safely as possible.

INTRODUCTION

Since Spring 2020 all WPAs have acted as crisis managers, a role that is not typically part of our professional training but that nonetheless is familiar to many WPAs. The COVID-19 global pandemic has caused over 681,341 deaths in the United States[1] with other significant effects including increased rates of unemployment, homelessness, and food insecurity, and decreased access to social support resources for medical care, mental health support, and childcare. The pandemic's effects have disparately impacted Black, Indigenous, and Latinx communities (García de Müeller et al., 2020). In addition to the pandemic, the unprosecuted murders of Black people by police have prompted national mass demonstrations to protest extrajudicial killing and to advocate for immediate antiracist and racial justice actions. These two concurrent crises have disrupted business as usual, and the crisis effects will shape higher education for years to come.

---

1. As of September 23, 2021, according to the *New York Times* (https://www.nytimes.com/interactive/2021/us/covid-cases.html).

WPAs have responded to the national crisis context through administrative, curricular, and pedagogical means. WPAs mobilized to shift instruction online, to adapt course curricula and pedagogical strategies, to troubleshoot technology and basic needs access for instructors and students, and to address racism in writing programs. Our professional response has required intense mental and emotional labor as we support instructors and students without the necessary information, time, and resources while also attending to our own personal precarity during an unprecedented global health, economic, and social crisis. This labor is exacerbated for Black WPAs and WPAs of color who must also contend with the dehumanizing effects of white supremacy and racism (Carter-Tod, 2020; Craig & Perryman-Clark, 2011, 2016; Kynard, 2019).

The global pandemic, widespread racial justice protests, and political unrest present an unusual moment of extreme crisis response for WPAs, who are experienced at managing smaller-scale professional crises. During more typical times, the discipline faces crises like the increase in exploitative labor practices and the perceived literacy crisis. In our local writing programs, we respond to budget, staffing, scheduling, enrollment, student, or instructor crises. But these are not the only crises that impact writing programs. Natural disasters, student or instructor deaths, campus shootings, and, more recently, pandemics, protests, and political coups are only some crisis situations that can disrupt the writing program's mission of teaching and learning about writing. WPAs respond to these less frequent crises, often without the appropriate training or procedures to ensure that we respond efficiently, effectively, and safely.

I quickly learned about the WPA's role in crisis management when the 1 October shooting took place three months after I started my WPA job at the University of Nevada, Las Vegas (UNLV). As WPA, I located writing program staff and faculty, shared institutional communications, identified campus and community resources, adjusted course curriculum, offered pedagogical accommodations, and supported instructors and students. None of my actions in the shooting aftermath were part of my job description, nor had I received any crisis training. My actions after the shooting were informed by my previous experiences with violence in educational settings. I have sheltered in place during lock-downs on every campus where I have studied and worked. I learned that a crisis can occur at any moment, and this knowledge has shaped my professional identity as a writing instructor and now a WPA. My personal history prepared me to act quickly after the Las Vegas shooting and more recently during the COVID-19 pandemic, but still I needed more preparation to support students, faculty, and myself during crisis situations.

Crisis management may not seem like a WPA's responsibility, especially when WPAs already have so much work related to our disciplinary expertise. Crisis management is not mentioned in the job categories presented in *The Portland Resolution* (Hult et al., 1992) or recognized as our professional intellectual labor (CWPA, 2019). Even though crisis management does not appear in our written position descriptions, WPAs are called to act as programmatic first responders in the event of an emergency (Clinnin, 2020). During a crisis, WPAs must transform an institution's emergency response efforts into practical writing program and classroom applications. The WPA's logistical, intellectual, and emotional labor is exacerbated by the lack of safety and stability. WPAs can reduce the mental and emotional burden of crisis response by proactively practicing crisis management so that in the event of an emergency we can respond efficiently, effectively, and safely on behalf of the writing program without neglecting our own care.

In this article, I demonstrate how WPAs can engage in the crisis management process to create crisis-ready writing programs. I introduce educational crisis management scholarship to define and identify writing program crises. Based on this scholarship and my crisis experience, I present a process that WPAs can use to prepare for, respond to, and recover from crisis situations. My hope is that this article will help WPAs practice crisis management to create writing programs that are safe and secure spaces for teaching and learning. And in the unfortunate event that a crisis has already occurred, the crisis evaluation process presented here can guide the WPA's immediate response and ongoing recovery efforts to support students, faculty, and administrators while also prioritizing the WPA's own well-being.

CRISIS MANAGEMENT IN EDUCATIONAL SETTINGS

Educators are increasingly responsible for crisis management due to the frequency of natural and human-caused crises; it is not a question *if* a crisis situation will occur but *when* (Cowan & Rossen, 2013, p. 8). In this section, I review educational crisis management scholarship and identify potential writing program crises. I then discuss ways that WPAs can collaborate with existing campus crisis management initiatives as a starting point for writing program crisis management.

The first step to creating a crisis-ready writing program is differentiating writing program crises from challenges. WPAs frequently encounter challenges and less frequently experience crises. Challenges and crises require different labor to respond appropriately and safely. Failure to differentiate a challenge from a crisis may lead to overreactions or inadequate responses with unintended consequences. For example, approaching all challenges as crises may put WPAs at risk of emotional burnout, which is already an occupational hazard present in many WPA narratives (Dardello, 2019; George, 1999; Keaton Jackson, 2018), whereas responding to crisis situations without proper training and procedures may result in insufficient responses that risk safety and security (Kerr, 2009; Knox & Roberts, 2005).

Crisis management scholarship defines a crisis as an event "that physically affects a system as a whole and threatens its basic assumptions, its subjective sense of self, its existential core" (Pauchant & Mitroff, 1992, p. 15). Crises are extraordinary situations with widespread physical and emotional impacts that require unusual practical and emotional labor to manage the situation (Zdziarski, 2007), whereas challenges are more limited in severity and scale. Many crises are beyond the WPA's professional responsibilities and abilities to manage, so instead WPAs should focus on educational crises, which are events on or off-campus that impact the institution, students, and faculty (Kerr, 2009). Educational crises disrupt the typical work of teaching and learning and cause physical, mental, and emotional distress for students and faculty. By limiting their concern to educational crises, WPAs do not need to respond to all crises but can focus their attention on the crises most likely to impact the writing program.

Next, WPAs should familiarize themselves with the existing educational crisis management strategies on their campus. The goal of educational crisis management is to ensure the immediate safety and security of students, faculty, and staff and to address long-term physical, logistical, mental, and emotional needs (Demaria & Schonfeld, 2013). As illustrated in figure 1, educational crisis management is an iterative process of prevention, preparation, response, and recovery (Cowan & Rossen, 2013). Prevention and preparation practices occur before a crisis. Prevention facilitates a safe and positive learning environment to reduce the likelihood of an avoidable crisis. Preparation establishes procedures for potential crises events and trains personnel to implement these procedures. Response occurs during a crisis situation to mitigate harm and re-establish physical safety and security. Finally, recovery is the ongoing effort to re-establish normalcy by attending to impacted individuals' short- and long-term physical, emotional, and material needs.

```
                    ┌─────────────────────────────────┐
                    │ Prevention: Actions that reduce │
                    │ likelihood of a crisis          │
                    │  • Creating a safe learning environment
                    │  • Funding campus safety infrastructure
                    │  • Establishing accessible mental health
                    │    resources                    │
                    └─────────────────────────────────┘
```

- **Prevention**: Actions that reduce likelihood of a crisis
  - Creating a safe learning environment
  - Funding campus safety infrastructure
  - Establishing accessible mental health resources

- **Recovery**: Actions that address short- and long-term needs
  - Identifying community partners
  - Providing emergency food, shelter, and funding
  - Adapting institutional policies and procedures (ex: registration, student fees)

- **Preparation**: Actions that establish crisis procedures
  - Forming a campus crisis response team
  - Developing campus crisis plans
  - Training personnel on procedures

- **Response:** Actions that mitigate harm and re-establish safety
  - Implementing crisis plan
  - Assisting authorities and emergency services
  - Communicating information to stakeholders

Figure 1. Higher education crisis management process and actions

Although educational institutions are federally-required to practice crisis management, campus efforts often fail to include writing program professionals or address crisis management within writing programs. Campus crisis-response training is typically mandated only for student affairs professionals and administrators. Academic faculty are unlikely to receive crisis management training, which can risk instructors' and students' safety during a crisis. Writing program instructors may be unaware of existing campus crisis procedures or how to access available crisis training. Furthermore, campus crisis plans often focus on campus-wide efforts to re-establish safety and limit physical harm rather than individual actions. Campus crisis plans do not address how WPAs and writing instructors can practice prevention, preparation, response, and recovery actions within their roles, leaving individuals to determine appropriate actions during a crisis.

To ensure the safety of administrators, instructors, and students, writing programs need their own crisis management practices that supplement existing campus crisis management protocols. WPAs can establish crisis-ready writing programs by collaborating with existing campus crisis management providers and then developing writing program crisis practices that address crisis prevention, preparation, response, and recovery. Engaging in this crisis-management process will help WPAs establish the writing program as a positive educational environment that may prevent potential crises and help re-establish learning after a crisis. These proactive steps will make the WPA position more sustainable in a crisis by reducing some of the practical, mental, and emotional labor.

Preventing Crises by Establishing Positive Writing Program Climates

The crisis management process begins with prevention to establish a positive educational climate that meet students and professionals' social, mental, and emotional needs. A positive educational climate is characterized by healthy relationships among school personnel, students, and their families; teachers and staff trained to recognize and respond to emotional distress in students; and access to mental health resources (Cowan & Rossen, 2013; Kerr, 2009). A positive educational climate cannot eliminate all potential crisis situations, but it can facilitate more effective crisis response and recovery because school personnel will be prepared to meet students' changing safety, social, emotional, and academic needs. However, school personnels' socioemotional needs must also be met for personnel to address students' needs after a crisis (Devine, 2007). School personnels' needs warrant special consideration given the high rates of teacher attrition attributed to high-stress working environments (Brasfield, Lancaster, & Xu, 2019) and the emotional labor associated with teaching, which contributes to burnout, compassion fatigue, and vicarious trauma (Skovholt, 2016). School administrators can mitigate some of this professional stress by recognizing emotional and mental wellness issues in the workplace and creating structures that support holistic wellness (Brasfield, Lancaster, & Xu; Grayson & Alvarez, 2008). Establishing a positive educational environment before a crisis provides students and personnel with the socioemotional support needed for recovery.

Although the research connecting a positive educational climate to crisis management has emerged from K-12 settings, WPAs can apply these findings to create positive writing program climates. A positive writing program climate recognizes emotional labor and values self-care. One strategy to create a healthy writing program climate is to encourage program personnel to develop self-care plans to maintain their mental, emotional, and physical wellness. Individuals in high-stress occupations like emergency first responders who use self-care plans are less likely to suffer from professional burnout and more likely to respond to workplace stress appropriately (Mastracci, Guy, & Newman, 2012). Although writing professionals' labor differs from that of emergency responders', even under normal working conditions writing professionals are at-risk of professional burnout and can benefit from practices like self-care plans. Self-care practices become even more important during a crisis as the typical emotional labor of college writing instructors and administrators substantially increases (Borrowman, 2005; DeBacher & Harris-Moore, 2016; Hodges Hamilton, 2016). Self-care can be incorporated into ongoing writing program professional development through discussions of the emotional dimension of our work and the importance of self-care. Discussing self-care does not eradicate structural issues that exacerbate faculty stress and burnout, but it can help to establish the writing program as a professional space where we care about students *and* instructors' well-being.

Writing professionals can create more positive educational climates by training in psychological first aid to support students' mental health. Psychological first aid helps instructors recognize students' social, emotional, and mental needs and connect students to relevant resources (Ready.gov, n.d.). College writing instructors may not learn about students' physical, mental, social, and emotional development as part of their professional training, so psychological first aid training can benefit students and instructors. Psychological first aid can help instructors address common mental health concerns that may appear in student interactions or writing, and in a crisis, the same psychological first aid techniques will help instructors respond appropriately to students' needs. WPAs can offer psychological first aid training as an ongoing professional development opportunity. Psychological first aid training is available through national organizations, but even collaborating with the local counseling center to facilitate a conversation about students' mental, social, and emotional needs and to compile local resources can help instructors better support students at all times.

Writing program prevention actions thus include

- Recognizing emotional labor as part of administrative and instructional labor
- Discussing emotional labor during program professional development and meetings
- Encouraging instructors and WPAs to practice self-care
- Offering psychological first aid training for instructors and administrators to assist students

Preparing for Crisis by Developing
Program Crisis management Plans

While crisis prevention attempts to stop a crisis from occurring by establishing a positive educational climate, crisis preparation ensures that all stakeholders have the necessary knowledge and skills to respond quickly, effectively, and safely in a crisis. WPAs can initiate crisis preparation by creating crisis management plans and educating program faculty on their responsibilities during a crisis.

Writing program crisis preparation begins with learning about existing campus crisis response personnel and plans. Institutions are federally mandated to develop and routinely review campus crisis response plans. These plans provide "clarity and consistency in how the campus addresses a crisis" and reduce "confusion or debate on key issues that might arise in the heat of the moment" (Zdziarski, 2007, p. 74). The campus crisis response plan provides instructions to address potential emergencies like fires, hazardous material spills, medical emergencies, and even elevator malfunctions. As noted in the prevention stage, WPAs should review the campus crisis-response plans and share these plans with program instructors so that all writing program personnel can follow local crisis procedures.

Campus crisis response plans present procedures to re-establish physical safety and security during various crises, but there are some limitations that require WPAs to develop supplemental writing program crisis response plans to guide programmatic actions during a crisis. Campus response plans address crises that impact the safety and security of campus or that require assistance from local authorities, but these plans do not address all potential disruptive events or include all university personnel. The campus response plans may not address smaller-scale crises such as the death of an instructor, or administrators may decide that a crisis does not warrant a campus response. Furthermore, crisis response plans do not involve all university personnel who may need to act in crisis situations. The intended audience for most campus crisis response plans are the emergency professionals responsible for decision making, coordinating efforts, and communicating information during a crisis. Campus crisis response plans are not designed for non-emergency campus professionals like WPAs and instructors, and as a result, the crisis response plans do not address non-emergency crisis response actions. However, non-emergency professionals must still make decisions during crises about if and how to carry out their professional responsibilities. For example, without guidance from the campus crisis response team, writing instructors must decide whether to hold class or how to accommodate students' learning needs during a crisis. WPAs can address these gaps by creating supplemental writing program crisis management plans that can guide writing program faculty's actions during a crisis.

The process of creating a writing program crisis management plan begins with anticipating the crises that are most likely to disrupt the writing program's teaching and learning mission and proactively establishing response and recovery actions. A writing program crisis management plan establishes procedures that ensure the safety and security of students and instructors, the effective communication of information, and the necessary support during and after a crisis event. Proactively developing a writing program crisis management plan relieves some of the logistical labor and emotional burden that WPAs may experience during a crisis. In my own experience after the 1 October shooting, I was overwhelmed by the responsibility of making programmatic decisions and guiding instructors while also processing my own emotional reaction to the shooting, a reaction made more complicated by my previous experiences with gun and campus violence. After the shooting, I developed writing program crisis materials for future use. I was able to adapt these materials in Spring 2020 as part of the writing program COVID-19 response, which reduced my own cognitive and emotional labor amidst a global crisis.

Developing a writing program crisis management plan is a multi-step process[2]. First, WPAs should familiarize themselves with campus crisis personnel and procedures. WPAs can collaborate with campus crisis personnel while developing the writing program crisis management plan to ensure the plan aligns with campus emergency management efforts and complies with legal mandates. After reviewing existing plans, WPAs can identify likely writing program crises that may not be covered by the institution's broader crisis response measures. Some disruptive events may include the death of a student or instructor, campus protests, hate speech, and campus violence. WPAs can imagine the potential effects of each crisis situation by answering the following questions:

- Who/what is involved (students, faculty, administrators, classroom spaces, etc.)?
- What impact does the crisis have on those involved (physical, mental, emotional, pedagogical, infrastructural, etc.)?
- What will those involved need in the short-term to feel safe and secure?
- What will those involved need in the long-term to return to normalcy?

---

2. A writing program crisis management plan template is available at https://bit.ly/wpacmplan for those readers who would like to create a plan for their own writing program.

- How can the writing program respond to these needs?

The answers to these questions provide the foundation of a writing program crisis management plan.

Once the WPA has identified possible crises, they can develop writing program crisis communication and response procedures. Crisis communication protocols identify who will communicate information to writing program personnel. Other campus offices may handle crisis communication due to federal guidelines for student privacy (FERPA) and timely notification of safety risks (the Clery Act), so WPAs should communicate specific information about the writing program's administrative, pedagogical, and curricular response actions, which are discussed more later in this article. WPAs can also share campus and local resources that can provide support during and after crises. Although each crisis event will require WPAs to analyze the situation for specific impacts and necessary actions, this proactive process of crisis analysis and preparation will help WPAs safely and efficiently address stakeholders' needs during a crisis.

A writing program crisis management plan is only as effective as the training provided to writing program personnel to use the plan and to act accordingly. Instructors recognize their lack of training for crisis situations (Borrowman, 2005; DeBacher & Harris-Moore, 2016). Training can help WPAs and instructors feel more confident in their ability to act swiftly and safely should a crisis ever occur (Brock et al., 2016). This training may be provided through in-person workshops, online modules, or compiled resources. Training events are opportunities for WPAs to collaborate with other campus and community entities on writing programs crisis preparation. Collaborative training events help campus offices understand writing program work so that they can better support instructors and students, and these events also help instructors understand their crisis management role. For example, campus emergency services may lead a training session on fire and evacuation procedures in the classroom buildings most frequently used by writing courses, or the counseling center can suggest discussion facilitation strategies for emotional topics. At my institution, I have addressed the immediate need for more crisis training by compiling resources for instructors including a handout from our counseling services about working with students in distress, a script for leading class after crisis events, and contact information for campus resources that provide emergency, counseling, and legal services. The resources are available on a program resource site so that instructors can access information at any time, and I also share these resources with program instructors as needed after a crisis. In the long-term, I plan to incorporate a crisis management session in our yearly orientation for program instructors and as a class session in the required practicum course for new graduate teaching instructors. These are low-effort ways to provide instructors with important training that can reduce their logistical, pedagogical, and emotional labor during a crisis situation without adding more uncompensated labor to their already excessive workload.

Writing program preparation actions thus include

- Familiarizing yourself with your institution's campus crisis-response team and plan
- Developing a writing program crisis management plan that aligns with the institutional crisis management process
- Maintaining updated contact information for all writing program instructors
- Compiling relevant crisis resources for instructors
- Providing training to instructors on possible writing program crisis situations

Responding to Crisis by Evaluating and Acting

Building on prevention and preparation, crisis response directly addresses the crisis situation to re-establish safety and security. In any crisis situation, the WPA's first responsibility is to follow the existing campus crisis management plan and instructions provided by campus or local authorities. However, these campus-wide plans and directions will not address all of the concerns of writing program stakeholders, so WPAs must supplement campus crisis response by providing writing program crisis response. Ideally, WPAs will follow the existing crisis management plan developed during crisis preparation and make necessary adjustments to respond to the specific crisis. In the following section, I suggest ways that WPAs can evaluate crises and take safe, effective, efficient, and role-appropriate actions.

Writing program crisis response begins by evaluating the crisis' scope and effects to determine an appropriate response. Crisis responders evaluate situations according to type, level, stakeholders, and effects (Zdziarski, 2007), and WPAs can use the categories presented in figure 2 to evaluate writing program crises. Type identifies the crisis' cause, which may be environmental, logistical, or human. Level refers to the crisis' scale and can range from the relatively-small scale like a classroom to an entire institution or a local community. Stakeholders are those who are directly or indirectly impacted by the crisis event. Effects are the short- and long-term impacts from the crisis.

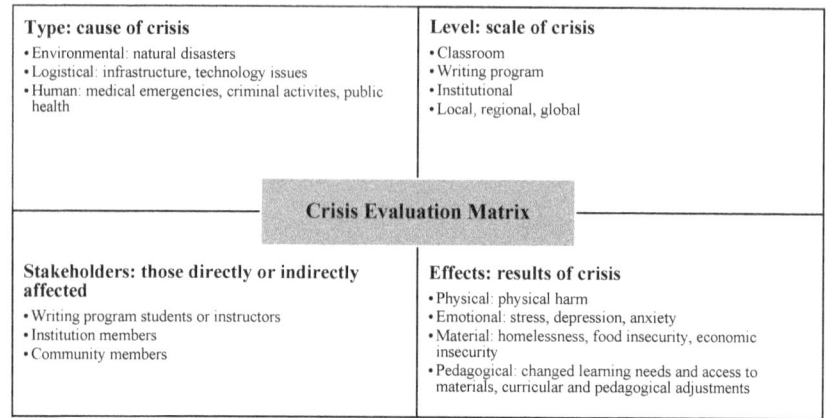

Figure 2. WPA Crisis Evaluation Matrix

Although it is impossible to anticipate all aspects of a crisis, the crisis evaluation process can help WPAs systemically analyze what is often a confusing and chaotic situation to guide their actions during crisis management.

In addition to the existing crisis evaluation categories, WPAs should also consider agency, or their ability to respond to a crisis. The WPA's agency may be constrained by the crisis context and other institutional actors. Crisis response highlights the WPA's liminal position within the institution; there are some crises for which WPAs are primarily responsible because the crisis impacts only the writing program or there is no institutional response, but in other situations there may be a unified campus crisis response. As part of their crisis analysis process, WPAs should evaluate their agency by identifying the other institutional actors that may make decisions that affect the writing program. During a crisis, WPAs may need to wait for these institutional actors to provide instructions or policies before the WPA can proceed with writing program crisis response.

To demonstrate how WPAs can use the crisis evaluation matrix, I present my evaluation process to determine my program's COVID-19 response in March 2020. COVID-19 is a multifaceted crisis that WPAs cannot respond to completely, but we can treat the pandemic as an educational crisis to evaluate its effects on students and instructors in the writing program to determine appropriate programmatic responses. The crisis type was an ongoing human, public health crisis. The crisis level was global, but by reframing the pandemic as an educational crisis, I focused on the writing program and writing classrooms. The primary crisis stakeholders within the writing program were the 5,000 students enrolled in writing courses and

100 contingent instructors teaching in Spring 2020. Each of these stakeholders experienced different effects from the pandemic. All stakeholders had a potential physical impact; anyone could be exposed to COVID-19 or test positive, although some individuals were at greater risk due to their health history. Basic needs could not be assumed as many individuals faced increased housing, food, and economic insecurity. Stakeholders experienced ranging emotional effects including grief, trauma, anger, depression, burnout, and fatigue as the pandemic continued. The pandemic disrupted any sense of safety and security, and the campus closed as a public health precaution. All students and instructors needed information about how the spring semester would continue. Although the university announced the physical closure of campus, this institutional response did not address all concerns. Instructors needed to "pivot" their classes to emergency remote instruction, and students needed to adapt to an entirely online course-load. Not all instructors or students had access to computers, Internet, course materials, or suitable workspaces off-campus. In addition to the emotional and material concerns, writing program instructors needed pedagogical guidance. A majority of the instructors had never taught online before, so the shift to emergency remote instruction with only one week of preparation presented a significant technological and curricular challenge. Finally, my agency in this crisis was constrained. I did not have the authority to move all writing courses to a remote format until the institution closed campus, and writing program policies regarding instructor and student health, technology access, and course grades needed to align with still-developing institutional policies. I did have the agency to respond to stakeholders' needs by offering logistical, curricular, and pedagogical support.

After evaluating the crisis, WPAs will be in a better position to decide how to respond safely, effectively, and efficiently, often in collaboration with other campus entities. For example, WPAs may need to work with campus offices to relocate classroom spaces, find new instructors for short or long-term need, adjust program policies for adding, dropping, or withdrawing from courses, and adjust to any university changes to the academic calendar. WPAs may also need to communicate information from campus crisis management personnel to program instructors. Although campus authorities communicate information to campus members, these messages may be generic and unable to address instructors' immediate concerns. In a study of contingent faculty teaching after Hurricane Sandy, Carl Schlachte found that instructors wanted more guidance from the writing program; the absence of program directives meant that most of the instructors felt that they did not know how to respond to the natural disaster appropriately or did not feel authorized to make changes to their classes (2020). With

Schlachte's findings in mind, WPAs can approach crisis communication as an opportunity to provide specific information and support to writing instructors. WPAs can establish the tone for crisis response by recognizing the crisis situation, validating the experience and response that individuals may have to the crisis, conveying accurate information as needed, providing clear instructions for instructors' roles and responsibilities, and sharing resources (Demaria & Schonfeld, 2013). WPAs can suggest appropriate pedagogical responses or authorize instructors to be flexible. Pedagogical response may range from course-management issues like modifying course curriculum or adjusting attendance policies and deadlines to student support concerns like working with distressed students and facilitating class discussions after a crisis. WPA crisis response should help program stakeholders understand their responsibilities, access relevant resources, and feel supported during an uncertain time.

My response in March 2020 to the COVID-19 pandemic focused on providing logistical and pedagogical information to instructors. Like all crisis management situations, leading the writing program pandemic response was intellectually, emotionally, and physically exhausting, compounded by the fact that I was nine months pregnant. My physical vulnerability heightened my perceived risk to students and instructors if in-person instruction continued. My impending leave accelerated the need to initiate writing program crisis response procedures for the immediate crisis situation (an anticipated fast move to remote instruction) and future effects such as fall scheduling changes. My administrative labor was reduced because I had already developed crisis response procedures and resources that I could adapt for this context. At the time it was unclear whether the university would continue in-person instruction or shift to remote, so I created contingency plans for both scenarios. I drafted a COVID-19 plan for the writing program administrative team that established our process for supporting instructors and students whether instruction continued in-person or online; the internal plan helped us collaboratively address the aspects within our control, identify gaps in instructor and student support that we could rectify, delegate responsibilities, and ensure continuity in our writing program operations. A major concern was how to ensure instructional continuity regardless of the university's decision about delivery format. I created a pedagogical guide that presented ways instructors could quickly adapt their classes for emergency remote instruction. The guide was by no means comprehensive, but it provided instructors with clear priorities and manageable actions that they could take to move their class online. Our writing program team was especially concerned about how the shift to remote instruction would impact our entirely contingent instructor population and drastically increase their workload while they also dealt with personal pandemic effects. We surveyed our instructor population about their ability to teach remotely and what they needed to do so successfully. We created extensive curricular materials such as modified course schedules, online course content, and course shells for the learning management system so that instructors could use these materials as a starting point for their now-remote class. Our team hosted several drop-in help sessions for instructors to ask questions about teaching remotely, to receive individual technical help, and to maintain human connection during social isolation. I also provided several resources about teaching during a crisis, trauma-informed pedagogy, self-care, and a list of campus and local resources for emergency financial support, food insecurity, homelessness, mental health support, and health care access.

Our writing program response did not eradicate all of the damage and trauma from the COVID-19 crisis, but our response did ease some of the burden for our instructors and students. Instructors shared that they felt personally and professional supported by our comprehensive writing program. Our response to this crisis and all of the procedures, documents, and resources that we have created and compiled will inform our future crisis response. We have continued to re-evaluate the crisis and our stakeholder needs so that we can effectively respond as the pandemic context changes, and, eventually, begin the recovery process.

Writing program response actions thus include

- Analyzing the crisis event according to type, level, stakeholders, and effects to determine appropriate response
- Recognizing the limits and possibilities of your ability to respond to the crisis
- Collaborating with other campus offices as needed
- Communicating usable, relevant information to writing program stakeholders
- Re-evaluating the ongoing situation to identify kairotic response actions

Recovering from Crisis by Supporting and Accommodating

Crisis recovery is the ongoing process of returning to normalcy and usual functions after the crisis event is resolved (Cowan & Rossen, 2013). Recovery builds on response activities by extending these efforts into the future. During the recovery stage, writing program stakeholders return to the educational setting and re-start the work of teaching and learning about writing, but long-term crisis effects may continue to impact this work. WPAs can be prepared to assist in the recovery process by attending to students' and instructors' ongoing mental, emotional, and pedagogical needs.

Mental and emotional wellness are major considerations during crisis recovery as impacted individuals must heal from the crisis event and resume daily routines. The proactive strategies from the crisis prevention stage that establish an emotionally healthy educational environment for students and personnel are foundational to crisis recovery. After a crisis, strategies such as continued use of self-care plans can aid in the mental and emotional recovery process. However, the same preventative strategies used before a crisis may no longer be as effective due to trauma caused by crises, so additional recovery tools may be needed to address impacted individuals' new mental and emotional needs. One such tool is episodic critical incident stress management. First-responders use critical incident stress (CIS) debriefings facilitated by a counselor to process crisis events, which involve discussing their professional actions in the crisis and sharing their emotional reactions (Mastracci, Guy, & Newman, 2012). CIS debriefings are opportunities for personnel to discuss the effectiveness of procedures and their actions and to suggest revisions to procedures or practices for future scenarios. CIS debriefings also destigmatize the emotional dimensions of work. During these sessions, personnel discuss their emotional responses to the crisis event and develop effective coping mechanisms that may reduce burnout and vicarious trauma (43). Although writing program stakeholders are unlikely to experience the same trauma as emergency first responders, collaborating with local counseling resources to facilitate a similar discussion after a crisis can benefit writing program stakeholders' recovery process. If campus or community resources are unavailable, even sharing information about stress reactions to trauma may help writing program personnel be more likely to recognize their own emotional responses, to seek help if needed, and to direct others to available resources.

Instructors will also need to support students through the crisis recovery process by engaging in pedagogical recovery practices that can accommodate students' changing educational needs. After a crisis, students may have difficulty focusing, retaining course material, and attending class regularly (Davidson, 2017; Sitler, 2009) They may express out-of-character emotions like anxiety, fear, and anger, or they may isolate themselves (Davidson, 2017; Sitler, 2009). Writing program instructors who are prepared to provide psychological first aid can recognize these signs and support student recovery by helping students access needed resources and adapting the learning environment as necessary. Trauma-informed pedagogy suggests that instructors empower students by allowing them to make decisions about their learning so that they feel a sense of control and agency (Davidson, 2017). For example, allowing students to make decisions about project deadlines is a small way that students can control part of their lives without abandoning the structure that is needed after a crisis event. It may also be appropriate to review course content and assignments, and, if necessary, to provide content warnings or alternative assignments so that students who may be distressed by the content can participate in other ways. While these may seem like small adjustments that align with effective pedagogy at all times, it is important that WPAs present these trauma-informed pedagogical practices to the writing program instructors during the crisis recovery process. Instructors may not feel empowered to make changes to the set curriculum, or they may be unsure about appropriate actions given the crisis. Partly this is a matter of preparing instructors for crisis and trauma-informed pedagogies in advance, but WPAs can mitigate some instructor anxiety by reminding instructors of appropriate classroom accommodations and existing resources to support students during a difficult time.

Providing pedagogical recovery practices was one of my most important contributions as WPA after the 1 October shooting. Instructors required a space to process how the shooting impacted their professional responsibilities and help to determine appropriate short- and long-term classroom responses. To address these needs for emotional support and professional guidance, I organized a critical incident stress debriefing that was well-attended by program graduate teaching assistants and part-time instructors. I requested that two counselors from our university center attend to help instructors process their own response to the shooting and to provide strategies for working with students after a trauma. With the counselors' assistance, I led a discussion about the shooting's impact on our work as writing instructors, including our responsibilities to support students and the limits to the support we could provide in our role. Instructors left the session understanding how to recognize signs of trauma that they and their students may exhibit over the coming weeks, how to adapt their classroom activities to accommodate students' needs, and what resources were available on campus and locally to assist affected individuals. The meeting did not resolve all of the questions or problems about teaching after a mass shooting, but it did initiate a dialogue about these concerns that helped instructors to feel more emotionally supported in the writing program and more confident in their professional response to students' needs after the tragedy. Our program has not yet addressed pedagogical recovery for COVID-19 as we are still actively in the response stage, but when we eventually do begin the recovery process, we will use similar trauma-informed strategies in the program and classrooms.

Writing program recovery actions thus include

- Continuing effective self-care strategies or adopt new self-care practices
- Collaborating with local mental health resources to provide a space for instructors to process their experiences and feelings as related to their professional role
- Offering trauma-informed pedagogical strategies to support student learning after a crisis

Next Steps to Creating Crisis-Ready Writing Programs

Throughout this article, I have presented a crisis management process as a way for WPAs to create crisis-ready writing programs. Crisis management is a contextual process that depends on the crisis as well as our own institutional and writing program structures, policies and procedures, personnel, and resources. The proactive process of preventing, preparing for, responding to, and recovering from crisis helps WPAs to learn more about their institutional crisis procedures and the needs of the program instructors and students before and after a crisis. As part of this process, WPAs will determine what crisis management practices are most effective for their program context.

There are many reasons why WPAs may be hesitant to engage in writing program crisis management. WPAs may feel overwhelmed by the labor needed to prepare for a crisis, unprepared by our professional training to manage a crisis, and frightened by the worst possible scenarios. Additionally, crisis management may be distressing for WPAs, particularly Black WPAs, WPAs of color, and WPA with histories of trauma. Crises do not impact everyone equally. Preparing for crisis is a stark reminder of how racism and white supremacy, sexism, ableism, classism, and other entrenched forms of discrimination exacerbate crisis situations for vulnerable communities. Crisis response and recovery resources are unequally distributed, and the relationship between crisis response human resources (police, medical services, mental health practitioners) and the communities they are intended to serve may be fraught. WPAs may find writing program crisis management difficult when they perceive a greater threat to their personal physical, mental, and emotional well-being. These are valid concerns that must be reckoned with as part of crisis management. While eradicating racism and discrimination in crisis management is beyond my capabilities to solve, the process approach to crisis management that I advocate throughout this article can alleviate some of the practical, mental, and emotional burden for WPAs. Crisis management works best as an ongoing, collaborative, programmatic initiative. By establishing crisis management plans in advance, WPAs can work with campus and community resources to develop relationships and to create equitable crisis response procedures that do not further expose vulnerable communities to more policing, surveillance, or harm. Proactive crisis management is also a worthwhile endeavor for individual WPAs to reduce their own practical, mental, and emotional labor during a crisis; with the writing program response planned in advance, the WPA can prioritize their personal well-being knowing that their professional responsibilities are handled.

Although crisis management is most beneficial when approached as an ongoing process, WPAs can begin the process with small actions that can have big impacts on the writing program's crisis readiness. First, educate yourself about campus policies and emergency personnel. Locate and read the campus emergency response plan. Make a copy easily accessible to instructors through an instructor resource site, a link on the writing program website, physical copies in instructor offices, or in orientation materials. Review these documents periodically to refresh your understanding and to stay updated on any policy changes. Establish relationships with relevant campus support units like campus safety and counseling center. These offices can provide specific information about how writing programs and instructors can better support emergency efforts and students during a potential crisis event, and depending on their own resources, they may be able to provide training for the writing program. And finally, start discussing role-specific crisis management as part of writing program administration and instruction work. Conversations about crisis response should not be limited to single training sessions but instead should be staged regularly. Talking about our professional roles during a crisis naturalizes crisis management so that it is a known professional responsibility that administrators and instructors are prepared for if a crisis does occur. Taking these relatively small actions before a crisis happens will set the foundation for later, more extensive crisis management actions and ultimately can help WPAs, instructors, and students be better prepared and safer in a crisis event.

References

Borrowman, S. (2005). *Trauma and the teaching of writing*. SUNY Press.

Brasfield, M. W., Lancaster, C., & Xu, Y. J. (2019). Wellness as a mitigating factor for teacher burnout. *Journal of Education, 199*(3), 166–178. https://doi.org/10.1177/0022057419864525

Brock, S.; Nickerson, A.; Louvar Reeves, C.; Conolly, S.; Jimerson, R. Pesce; & Lazzaro, B. (2016). *School crisis prevention and intervention: The PREPaRE Model* (2nd ed.). National Association of School Psychologists.

Carter-Tod, S. (2020). Administrating while black: Negotiating the emotional labor of an African-American female WPA. In C. Adams Wooten, J. Babb,

K.M. Costello, & K. Navickas (Eds.), *The things we carry: Strategies for recognizing and negotiating emotional labor in writing program administration* (pp. 197–214). Utah State University Press.

Clinnin, K. (2020). And So I Respond: The Emotional Labor of Writing Program Administrators in Crisis Response. In C. Adams Wooten, J. Babb, K.M. Costello, & K. Navickas (Eds.), *The things we carry: Strategies for recognizing and negotiating emotional labor in writing program administration* (pp. 129–144). Utah State University Press.

CWPA. (2019). *Evaluating the intellectual work of writing administration*. http://wpacouncil.org/aws/CWPA/pt/sd/news_article/242849/_PARENT/layout_details/false

Cowan, K. C., & Rossen, E. (2013). Responding to the Unthinkable: School Crisis Response and Recovery. *Phi Delta Kappan*, 95(4), 8–12. https://doi.org/10.1177/003172171309500403

Craig, C.L., & Perryman-Clark, S.M. (2011). Troubling the boundaries: (De)Constructing WPA identities at the intersections of race and gender. *WPA: Writing Program Administration*, 34(2), 37–58.

—. (2016). Troubling the boundaries revisited: Moving towards change as things stay the same. *WPA: Writing Program Administration*, 39(2), 20–27.

Dardello, A. (2019). Breaking the silence of racism and bullying in academia: Leaning in to a hard truth. In C.L. Elder & B.A. Davila (Eds.), *Defining, locating, and addressing bullying in the WPA workplace* (pp. 102–123). University Press of Colorado.

Davidson, S. (2017). *Trauma-informed practices for postsecondary education: A guide*. Education Northwest.

DeBacher, S., & Harris-Moore, D. (2016). First, do no harm: Teaching writing in the wake of traumatic events. *Composition Forum*, 34.

Demaria, T., & Schonfeld, D. J. (2013). Do it Now Short-Term Responses to Traumatic Events. *Phi Delta Kappan*, 95(4), 13–17. https://doi.org/10.1177/003172171309500404

Devine, J. (2007). *Making your school safe: Strategies to protect children and promote learning*. Teachers College Press.

García de Müeller, G., Cortes, A., Gonzales, L., Hanson, A., Jackson, C., Kahn, S., Lopez, B.E., & Simmons, B. (2020). Combating white supremacy in a pandemic: Antiracist, anticapitalist, and socially just policy recommendations in response to COVID-19. *The Journal of Multimodal Rhetorics*. http://journalofmultimodalrhetorics.com/combating-white-supremacy-in-a-pandemic-antiracist--anticapitalist--and-socially-just-policy-recommendations-in-response-to-covid-19

George, D. (Ed.). (1999). *Kitchen cooks, plate twirlers, & troubadours: Writing program administrators tell their stories*. Boynton/Cook Publishers.

Grayson, J.L., & Alvarez, H.K. (2008). School climate factors relating to teacher burnout: A mediator model. *Teaching and Teacher Education*, 24(5), 1349–1363. https://doi.org/10.1016/j.tate.2007.06.005

Hodges Hamilton, A. (2016). First responders: A pedagogy for writing and reading trauma. In M.J. Casper & E. Wertheimer (Eds.), *Critical trauma studies: Understanding violence, conflict and memory in everyday life* (pp. 179–204). NYU Press.

Hult, C., Jolliffe, D.A., Kelly, K., Mead, D., & Schuster, C. (1992). The Portland resolution: Council of writing program administrators guidelines for writing program administrator (WPA) positions. *WPA: Writing Program Administration, 16*(1–2), 88–94.

Keaton Jackson, K. (2018). A state of permanent transition: Strategies for WPA survival in the ever-present marginal space of HBCUs. In C. Adams Wooten, J. Babb, K.M. Costello, & K. Navickas (Eds.), *The things we carry: Strategies for recognizing and negotiating emotional labor in writing program administration* (pp. 25–36). Utah State University Press.

Kerr, M.M. (2009). *School crisis prevention and intervention*. Merrill/Pearson.

Knox, K.S., & Roberts, A.R. (2005). Crisis intervention and crisis team models in schools. *Children & Schools, 27*(2), 93–100. https://doi.org/10.1093/cs/27.2.93

Kynard, C. (2019). Administering while black: Black women's labor in the academy and the "position of the unthought." In S.M. Perryman-Clark & C.L. Craig (Eds.), *Black perspectives in writing program administration: From the margins to the center* (pp. 28–50). NCTE.

Mastracci, S.H., Guy, M.E., & Newman, M.A. (2012). *Emotional labor and crisis response: Working on the razor's edge*. M.E. Sharpe.

Pauchant, T.C., & Mitroff, I.I. (1992). *Transforming the crisis-prone organization: Preventing individual, organizational, and environmental tragedies*. Jossey-Bass.

Ready.gov. *Listen, protect, connect: Model & teach, psychological first aid (PFA) for students and teachers* (n.d.).

Schlachte, C. (2020). Shelter in place: Contingency and affect in graduate teacher training Courses. In C. Adams Wooten, J. Babb, K.M. Costello, & K. Navickas (Eds.), *The things we carry: Strategies for recognizing and negotiating emotional labor in writing program administration* (pp. 145–160). Utah State University Press.

Sitler, H.C. (2009). Teaching with awareness: The hidden effects of trauma on learning. *The Clearing House: A Journal of Educational Strategies, Issues and Ideas, 82*(3), 119–124. https://doi.org/10.3200/TCHS.82.3.119-124

Skovholt, T.M. (2016). *The resilient practitioner: Burnout and compassion fatigue prevention and self-care strategies for the helping professions* (3rd ed.). Routledge.

Zdziarski, E.L., Dunkel, N.W., & Rollo, J.M. (2007). *Campus crisis management: A comprehensive guide to planning, prevention, response, and recovery*. Jossey-Bass.

Kaitlin Clinnin is Assistant Professor of English and Director of Composition at the University of Nevada, Las Vegas. Her most recent research focuses on trauma-informed pedagogy in writing programs and classrooms. Her work has been published in *Computers & Composition, Composition Studies, Communications in Information Literacy,* and several edited collections including most recently *The Things*

We Carry: Strategies for Recognizing and Negotiating Emotional Labor in Writing Program Administration.

Vision and Visibility: A Call to Feminist WPAs

Casie Fedukovich

Abstract:

Grounded in the author's experience as a WPA overseeing GTA preparation during the 2016 Presidential election, this article explores feminist leadership as a methodology capable of fortifying and extending the work of writing program administration. By complicating the scope of WPA authority through various feminist- and leadership-informed strategies, the author proposes strategies intended to highlight the visionary potential feminist WPAs hold.

It is an important and challenging time to explicitly identify as a feminist Writing Program Administrator (WPA) and to envision how feminist principles might be enacted in our programs. Since the fall of 2016, many of us have been enmeshed in a deep personal and professional milieu that affects our teaching, our students' learning, and our program administration. Crude comments by then-presidential-candidate Donald Trump created a space where "locker room talk" objectifying women and supporting sexual assault was both authorized and accepted as typical, and in some circles, as a sign of masculinity. Concurrently, women's experiences have been brought to the fore through national conversations like the #MeToo movement, the Women's March on Washington in January 2017, Christine Blasey Ford's harrowing testimony regarding her sexual assault and the subsequent appointment of Brett Kavanaugh to the Supreme Court, the rollback of Title IX protections for victims of campus assaults, and ongoing debates regarding the overturn of Roe v. Wade.

In many cases, it is difficult to clearly and persuasively connect national discourse with local behaviors. That is, the effect of political rhetoric on public behavior is often too muddy to correlate. However, Trump's "locker room talk" soon became intertwined with the publicity of his campaign and then his new presidency. Merchandise rolled out. One could buy tee-shirts with any creative arrangement of his "locker room talk" emblazoned across the front. Overt misogyny became a popular and often-repeated political slogan, one that could be heard and viewed on city streets, in shopping centers, and in our classrooms.[1] As Kirsti Cole and Holly Hassel write, Trump's self-aggrandizing misogyny has left "[w]omen and girls… experiencing fear and strong negative emotions about their self-worth based solely on the Electoral College" (xvi).

It can feel like an insurmountable feat to approach our current moment as feminists, or as people who feel compelled to act in feminist-informed ways. A spring 2019 symposium of rhetoric and composition faculty and graduate students, edited by Michelle LaFrance and Elizabeth Wardle, called on WPAs to help "build a twenty-first-century feminist ethos," one that is intersectional and attends to radical inclusion (14). The editors summarize our uneasy times, recognizing the challenge in feeling like our feminist work "may . . . appear limited. Temporary. Isolated." And yet, they note, "[we] are talking about our experiences in ways we have not before" (31). It follows that making our struggles visible—through a social media movement like #MeToo, a disciplinary listserv, or by communicating situations in our individual programs in journal articles and at conferences—holds space for opportunities to foreground the feminist ethics we enact or wish to enact within our constrained administrative roles. To be a woman-identified WPA in 2020 is to keenly feel the pressure of national misogynistic discourse while also being responsible for managing its effects in our programs. WPAs, I contend, occupy a unique position to make this feminist-oriented work visible and valuable in their programs and more broadly on their campuses.

What follows is a discussion of the potential for feminist-informed leadership through writing program administration, framed in what I argue has been a local and national leadership vacuum in the aftermath of the election. While I am choosing to speak specifically about women-identified WPAs, I acknowledge that the practices I discuss are not gender-exclusive; however, the daily affective experiences of women will take the focus here, as I propose a model that considers gender as an organizing concept. In her landmark essay, "Becoming a Warrior," Louise Wetherbee Phelps reflects on her role as a new WPA, writing,

> What I had yet to learn, on the bones, was the circuit of devaluation that runs from women in general to women's work to composition as a feminized discipline and back to the concrete institutional project—the writing program as an enterprise, and its people. (297)

Currently, this "devaluation" operates in a crucible that includes explicitly protected and nationally authorized public displays of misogyny, which may be affecting the faculty and graduate students teaching in our programs, the students in our classes, and WPAs.

I propose feminist leadership as a methodology capable of informing, enriching, and fortifying Writing Program Administration during our tumultuous political moment. The competing needs of different constituencies create contradictions for feminist administrators, a phenomenon well traced through scholarship on "FemAdmin" in composition (Miller; Dickson; Jarratt and Worsham; Ratcliffe and Rickly; Reid; Goodburn and Leverenz). This article contributes to current conversations on the role of feminist and academic leadership in rhetoric and composition (Cole and Hassel; Adams Wooten, Babb, and Ray; Maimon) and offers options for approaching difficult situations for WPAs who may feel constrained to speak and act ethically. First, I contextualize my WPA experience through two defining narratives with women GTAs. I then move to discuss how we may extend the work of early FemAdmin scholars to develop strategies for feminist writing program leadership.

Setting the Scene: Woman WPA, Women GTAs

Like many writing program administrators, I began my career as an untenured WPA mentoring graduate teaching assistants, in charge of "mind[ing] the kids," while a tenured faculty member filled the more authoritative, and thus masculinized, role of program director (Reid 128). I held this position from August 2011 through July 2017, mentoring just over 150 GTAs to teach English 101: Academic Writing and Research, North Carolina State University's required first-year writing course. Fall 2016 quickly became a site of intensive "rescue mentoring" (Reid 131, 135), as I balanced preparing GTAs to teach critical thinking, effective communication, ethical use of sources, and information literacy against discussions of hate-speech protections, fake news, and real concerns about safety.

Our university is public, so institutional leaders were bound in their roles as representatives of the university to project political neutrality. This projection came down to the writing program as calls for civil discourse and unity and encouragement to our program faculty—all contingent instructors and GTAs—to help guide undergraduate students through difficult post-election discussions. It was a heavy task to place on the backs of our most insecurely employed and inexperienced faculty. Two experiences with women GTAs help illustrate some of these weedy administrative situations where I felt lost, even after five years in the position.

Early in the Fall 2016 semester, Megan, a 25-year-old GTA with no teaching experience, had disclosed that she recently experienced sexual violence.[2] She shared this information with me because she was still embroiled in the legal process, and public discourse and institutional conversations had left her feeling re-traumatized and anxious. Donald Trump's "locker room talk" came up in the teaching practicum, and I checked in with her frequently.

The day after the election, she appeared in my office door, visibly upset. A male student had worn a "Grab Her by the Pussy" shirt to class. Other students noticed and looked to Megan for a response. She explained to me that she was overcome with anxiety at his presence but chose to carry out that day's lesson without drawing attention to his shirt. After meeting with Megan, I called Student Conduct and our campus legal counsel, both of whom advised me that the student was protected in his choice to wear the shirt.

The undergraduate student's moment of celebration—which I felt pushed the boundaries of the student code of conduct—rocked Megan's confidence. In a little over three months into her teaching career, Megan had reached a point where she was so anxious that she became ill. She finished her teaching for the semester, grateful for the winter break.

The following spring, Amy, a 22-year-old GTA, met with me about a disruptive student. This male student had started openly criticizing her teaching and the content of the course, in a way that far surpassed reasonable feedback. It was a moment in class when Amy spoke about pronoun use in terms of trans* identities that this student grew agitated and berated both Amy and another female student. Other students approached Amy to say that this student made them feel uncomfortable speaking in class, as he would lash out with personal attacks. This student then submitted a reflection for a major assignment that only criticized the assignment, calling it, the class, and Amy "useless."

Of course, belligerent students are sometimes present in our first-year courses. We seat thousands of students, and a number of them express frustration with taking a required writing class, particularly at a STEM-focused institution. This student, however, behaved differently from past cases, both in tone and persistence. We looped in the Student Conduct Office. Amy notified the student that she was asking for help from another campus resource. He was quiet and cooperative in the next class, but this state was short-lived, as Amy returned graded assignments that day. The student failed the assignment. That evening, he sent Amy two more inflammatory emails.

Based on our feedback from Student Conduct, much of this student's issue with Amy appeared to be gendered and politically motivated. I spoke with Amy to ensure that her classroom discussions were balanced, focusing on the goal to de-escalate the student and the situation. Together, we crafted a plan that satisfied departmental expectations while taking into account the institution's operational definitions of terms like "disruption" and "harassment." After much discussion, I was advised that the student could not be placed in a different class unless or until he became physically disruptive or if his communication with her indicated a physical threat. Amy was bereft. This news meant that she had to continue to see this student multiple times a week and to potentially allow herself and others in the class to be subjected to his unpredictable behavior. Feeling overwhelmed, Amy focused her energy and finished out the semester, and the student passed the course. Amy, however, was emotionally drained. It was her last semester of graduate study. She had simultaneously been working to finish a demanding capstone project for graduation while teaching and planning for her next life choices. The experience caused her to ultimately reject college teaching as a future career.

Megan's and Amy's experiences illustrate the kind of complex negotiations WPAs may have encountered after the election. Conversations with WPAs at other institutions suggested that they were feeling likewise dislocated, as they related experiences with DACA students who had gone into hiding, students and faculty from the six "travel ban" countries afraid to leave the United States for fear they wouldn't be able to return, stories from students who had experienced taunts about "Trump's Wall," and a myriad of other identity-motivated attacks.

My experiences and the experiences of the WPA colleagues I backchanneled suggest that writing program administration was not immune from the "Trump Effect," a phenomenon the Southern Poverty Law Center defines as an uptick in bullying, hate crimes, and bias incidents against women, people of color, immigrants, religious minorities, and GLBTQIA people since Trump's election. WPAs may have found themselves caught in the middle, advocating for faculty and students while navigating institutional tangles that slowed resolution or exacerbated already bad situations. It was Laura Micciche's oft-cited "collective nervous condition in relation to WPA agency" come to life (77). As I experienced the election and its aftermath alongside the 21 GTAs I mentored during Fall 2016 and Spring 2017, our formal institutional relationship became inadequate in describing their needs and what I could provide. I could supervise on routine pedagogical processes, but I found myself feeling lost and unsure in this new political context, unable to efficiently or ethically solve their problems or answer their questions. In sending these new, vulnerable faculty into painful, frightening situations ostensibly supported by the university, I began to question my own ethics and fitness to serve as a WPA.

These problems were compounded by vague or non-committal institutional, college-level, and departmental guidance to maintain neutrality. For those of us in classrooms and who were responsible for supporting faculty who directly encountered hostility, messages of neutrality and civility felt inadequate (see Fedukovich and Doe). As each week brought new concerns, I quickly found the limits of my administrative identity as I had constructed it to that point. Further, I was a pre-tenure WPA at the time, and I had to account for how these overlapping relationships might affect my professional goals at my institution.

Leadership Vacuums through Constraint

For many WPAs, the aftermath of the election may have created situations that demanded careful ethical navigation and called us to step into unfamiliar roles. However, we may have felt constrained by perceptions of our role as managers of human resources, what other administrators consider our faculty and GTAs, and non-human resources: technology, space, materials. We keep students moving—into and out of our classes—remediate problems, handle complaints, and clean up pedagogical and logistical messes.

In academic settings, various "top leaders," positions such as provosts, chancellors, and deans, are looked to as visionaries for their institutions. They are often responsible for crafting and promoting important institutional texts like strategic plans and mission statements. These academic "top leaders" operate under different expectations than writing program administrators, yet they are likewise constrained (Mayfield, Mayfield, and Sharbrough). Like WPAs, they, too, answer to many audiences, including students, parents, and faculty, but also stakeholders like donors, local political bodies, and in my case at a state institution, the university system board and the public. The difference is proximity: Top-level leadership does not deal with the same daily realities of on-the-ground teaching, and this gap creates opportunities for communicative misfires such as those we perceived in my program. As Wendy Hesford's research determines, campus upheaval provides a dynamic, high-stakes environment for these types of communicative misfires to occur.

Hesford's exploration of a spate of racially-charged graffiti and cross burnings on Oberlin College's campus in the fall of 1993 provides one analysis of perceived inadequate campus leadership in the face of campus upheaval. She critiques Oberlin's administration's "color blind" responses to the events, as the official statement from the university's president "painted the image of Oberlin as a unified community" (141-42), a rhetorical move that devalued the effects explicit racism may have had on the campus community. Many students, faculty, and staff felt pain and fear in the aftermath of the events. Oberlin's president's insistence towards unity—from the safety of his powerful position—diminished these responses. Hesford proposes a view of the campus as a public space and a contact zone where pedagogical and administrative leadership might emerge to embrace the complexity of these discussions in order to move the community toward greater understanding and to signal support for those who may be afraid.

Research coming out of the 2016 elections echoes Hesford's frustrations with campus leaders making sense of crisis. McNaughtan, et al., analyze statements sent by presidents of 50 flagship public institutions after Trump's election. Using Lloyd Bitzer's definition of rhetorical situation, the researchers identify a complex and high-stakes post-election context for academic top leaders. Most of the university presidents (41 of 50) chose to send a public statement within the first two weeks after the election. Overall, many of these statements sought to "provide an institutional response to help students, faculty, and staff frame the election with regards to the national context of the election and its relationship to the objectives and culture of the university" (544). However, and pertinent to this discussion, 38 of the 41 statements called for unity "in an otherwise divided nation and campus" (539), and 35 called for "civility" and the promotion of "civil dialog" (541). Our experience at North Carolina State University was the rule, not the exception.

Like Hesford, McNaughtan, et al. identify campus leadership as insufficiently responding to crisis events. They write, "[W]hile public flagship institutions are political institutions, this should not prohibit them from responding to external events, even when political ramifications may be imminent" (545-46). Institutional top leaders were unable to communicate the gravity of the post-election situation in a way that reaffirmed their faculty, staff, and students' concerns. These constraints may have been perceived as a lack of clear and ethical leadership or, at the very least, as insensitive and naïve. In our first-year writing classroom, with its small sizes and focus on argument, complex situations arose that could not be addressed with blanket calls for civil discourse.

I am reminded of Amy's and Megan's struggles and of my administrative and ethical responsibility not only to their professional development but also to their personal safety and well-being. In the moment Megan appeared in my office doorway, overcome by anxiety triggered by her male student's sexually aggressive and presidentially endorsed tee-shirt, it did not seem appropriate to encourage her to seek unity with this student. Top leaders may have attempted to communicate in ways that, as the research suggests, upheld the election's "relationship to the objectives and culture of the university" (McNaughtan, et al., 544). WPAs understand this rhetorical move by campus administration as telling: The spaces we inhabit have always been exclusionary and dangerous for many of our students, faculty, and staff. Exclusion and danger *is* the culture of the modern American university. The 2016 election brought these experiences to us in urgent ways.

The Ideological Purity Trap

Scholarship on "FemAdmin" provides vocabulary and strategies to address these urgent problems, even as it complicates our understanding of what feminist approaches in program administration can achieve post-Trump. As an area of study, FemAdmin experienced increased attention through the 1990s, with foundational texts creating a shared sense for what this approach might look like. Feminist WPAs valued collaboration and eschewed top-down decision-making. Hierarchies were suspicious. The affective and cognitive could co-exist.

In detail, however, this emerging discussion was far more complex than a few named hallmark practices. Contradictions flourished, as feminisms-as-ideology engaged with realities of program administration. The false utopia of a fully feminist writing program complicates this early research, with scholars such as Louise Wetherbee Phelps and Hildy Miller recognizing that feminist approaches are often not the most appropriate or successful strategy in the masculinist institution. Miller encourages WPAs to think "bi-epistemologically," to "find ways to accommodate both masculinist and feminist models" in order to understand the rhetorical tools they have available and those best suited to the job (59). This assertion refuses ideological purity in favor of practical solutions. Rigidly holding to feminist principles, particularly when it is clear they will not be successful, may only create more problems.

Since the development of FemAdmin work 30 years ago, the research story of feminist writing program administration appears uneven and disconnected as a focus of study. Laura Micciche and Donna Strickland conclude their review of Krista Ratcliffe and Rebecca Rickly's key collection *Performing Feminism and Administration in Rhetoric and Composition* with the assertion that the text "give[s] evidence that many within the field still want to think about these possibilities, and still struggle to think beyond the apparent contradictions of such couplings" (175). The collection sought to provide an opportunity to "release the worries about contradictions and move toward new visions of feminist WPAing," and yet a decade later, we are still challenged to move "beyond oxymorons." Prior FemAdmin scholarship points out the contradictions inherent in dispensing administrative decisions without either the authority or support to make ethical, feminist-informed choices. Shifting focus to discuss possibilities for feminist leadership potential in writing program administration extends our options.

To be clear, this article cannot fully commit to Micciche and Strickland's call. Because of its limitations, it can provide only a pre-theoretical starting point for future feminist-informed writing program leadership research. This objective feels frustratingly inadequate for the task at hand. Every day seems to bring a new assault on our democratic underpinnings. Political and personal attacks on vulnerable populations continue.

The time is right, I argue, for this discussion to grow louder, more urgent, and more visibly informed by the many diverse voices in our discipline. What I intend to provide next is a discussion about how feminist leadership can extend our understanding of FemAdmin to complicate the WPA role broadly conceived and provide additional strategies WPAs might use in their individual programs.

The National Census of Writing suggests that women make up a majority of WPAs. Feminization, long held as composition's problem area as it indicated our lowly status, can be our strength. That is, women's experiences are, by sheer number, interlaced with composition's history and its current practices. Leveraging those experiences within an established framework of feminist thinking may provide a foothold in our ever-shifting administrative terrain. Women are the leaders writing program administration needs in this critical moment. Next, I broadly discuss ways in which feminist WPAs can begin or continue to develop recognition as visible leaders.

Leadership: Defining Terms, Extending Definitions

Because of perceived institutional leadership vacuums post-election, WPAs may have found themselves stepping into new, risky spaces. From my perspective as a pre-tenure WPA at the time, the feeling far exceeded administrative "plate twirling" (George) or the "manic, awkward dance" (Micciche 75) created by too many demands on a WPA's time. Instead, like many others, I was thrust into situations that implicated the immediate well-being of vulnerable people I was tasked to serve. The responsibility and consequences felt much greater than it had in prior semesters.

The field of composition has a long history of striving to meet ethical imperatives, and yet we still find ourselves mired in preconceptions about what a WPA is and can do. In turn, we may have found ourselves uneasily extending the scope of our roles or feeling conflicted with new problems that demanded leadership responses.

Here, I pause to delineate administration from leadership, two identities that WPAs experientially know to be different. Marlene G. Fine and Patrice Buzzanell, scholars in feminist leadership studies, carefully articulate the differences among and between three locations of practice—administration, management, and leadership—contending that the naming of these roles not only constrains how those in the role perceive their own authority but how others respond. Fine and Buzzanell write,

> Leadership is the process of externally articulating visions that challenge organizational identity and change; management is what translates that vision internally; and administration is the science of developing standardized and routine practices and constructs applicable to all members in every organization. (129)

In short, leaders are proactive and visionary, while administrators are reactive and constrained. Managers may straddle those identities, sometimes exhibiting the type of managerialism described by Donna Strickland and other times exhibiting managerial leadership, a process more closely tied to Fine and Buzzanell's definition of the manager as one responsible for carrying out visionary work in organizations.

Colleagues across campus and sometimes in our home departments often reduce the role of the WPA to its most obvious administrative components: the routine and mundane practices that define, per Fine and Buzzanell, an administrator. And while administrators and managers in this schema are given some influence through actions within their programs, they are often isolated from enacting visionary change. WPAs are thus known by their tasks: handling student complaints, scheduling courses, manipulating ever-decreasing budgets, preparing graduate students, hiring and reviewing faculty, and conducting assessment. These logistical tasks are written into job descriptions and enacted through daily to-do lists, and they comprise much of our scholarship in program administration.

To act as visionaries and leaders, WPAs must be invested with institutional authority. The question of WPA authority has long troubled the field. Shirley K Rose, Lisa S. Mastrangelo, and Barbara E. L'Eplattenier's 2013 update to Olsen and Moxley's earlier study on WPA authority concludes that "some conditions that were present in 1989 still persist and continue to hold writing program directors back from being able to garner sufficient authority to do their work effectively" (45). While Rose, Mastrangelo, and L'Eplattenier's research suggests that WPA agency can now be enacted in more diverse locations, many WPAs still find themselves caught in institutional tangles that foreclose visionary leadership work. Our current political landscape—including the overt demonstration of racist, xenophobic, and misogynistic beliefs—increases the administrative complexity, amplified by the necessity for immediate intervention and long-range planning.

Admittedly, it is unlikely that any approach to program administration would have changed the outcomes with the two women GTAs whose experiences opened this discussion. Their situations were so tightly bound in institutional logistics, including the university's need to appear politically neutral, that there was little room for alternatives. However, it has become clear in retrospect that their experiences indicate a new landscape for program administration, one that calls us to perform our feminist commitments in the face of the normalization of strong anti-feminist conditions. This landscape binds WPAs to those we serve in new ways that demand we recall, refresh, and amplify our feminist allegiances.

In the four years following Trump's election, public discourse about women's experiences has surged. National conversations such as #MeToo and the Kavanaugh hearings; the disciplinary listserv exchanges that prompted the LaFrance and Wardle symposium; and new texts such as Cole and Hassel's *Surviving Sexism in Academia: Strategies for Feminist Leadership*, Cristyn Elder and Bethany Davila's *Defining, Locating, and Addressing Bullying in the WPA Workplace*, and Shari Stenberg's *Repurposing Composition: Feminist Interventions for a Neoliberal Age* sound a clarion call for attention to women's experiences and, in turn, renewed attention to feminist approaches to our work.

Leadership as a primary WPA role has also recently emerged as an explicit focus of study in our disciplinary scholarship (Cole and Hassel; Adams Wooten, Babb, and Ray; Maimon), as the field works to understand what it could mean to be a WPA leader in our cultural and political context. Over the past 20 years, the landscape for feminist writing program leadership has clarified and been made more critical due to leadership vacuums and the ethical challenges of the moment. Next, I discuss strategic concepts that feminist WPA leaders might consider in their own programs. These concepts, of course, can only be enacted individually and are subject to local constraints. Recalling warnings against ideological purity (Miller; Phelps), I intend them to be scalable and practicable, in whole or part. Some may be enacted under the administrative radar, in small and quiet ways, while others require more secure visibility. They may coexist with masculinist approaches and still constitute a feminist approach to writing program leadership.

Building a Local Theory: The WPA as a Site of Ethical Action

Though feminist scholarship in writing program administration is wide ranging and varied, the concept of feminist responsibility to those we serve emerges as an ideological through-line. Wendy Bishop engages pastoral clericalism in encouraging WPAs to ask themselves three questions: "Whose cry do I hear? Toward whom do I move? Whose interests do I serve?" (352). In her article, "Theorizing Ethics in Writing Program Administration," Carrie S. Leverenz advances three areas for WPA focus: ethical awareness, ethical action, and ethical inquiry (111). Visibility is key to Leverenz's argument, as it forms the foundation on which writing program leadership can be productively and sustainably enacted as a serious ethical endeavor. Leverenz writes, "It seems clear that, as a profession, we have not done a good job of conveying the ethical import of this work to others within our institution or without" (113). In taking an earnest approach to ethics as an iterative social process shared among faculty and administrators, the WPA demonstrates her commitment to the people of the program beyond its logistical management.

A feminist approach to writing program administration first acknowledges program leadership as a site of ethical action; it may then move to include authority as a positive concept. Authority may implicate a WPA who acts alone, who does not seek equitable distribution of power in her program. As tenure lines continue to be replaced with non-tenured positions, the balance of security likewise shifts. Unless a writing program can support multiple protected and adequately compensated administrators, distributed administrative models could saddle insecure faculty with extra labor and risk. A feminist WPA acting as a solo programmatic leader thus becomes an ethical demonstration, in a recognition of other's precarious employment positions, low pay, and already high workload.

Louise Wetherbee Phelps identified this conundrum in 1995, just as rumblings of the dire-labor-situation-to-come started to emerge: If "as feminists, we are arguing for broadly distributed power and access, we must be prepared to imagine that one can ethically have visions, lead, and wield power, despite the imperfectability of institutions and the tragic limitations of human action" (293). In this way, the WPA-acting-alone can emerge as a steadying force in program leadership, facing institutional changes and constraints with a clear, ethical vision.

Laura Davies updates and extends this thinking to implicate power as a productive, not suspicious, construct in feminist program administration. WPAs, she writes, have an "ethical responsibility to use their expertise and authority proactively toward a particular purpose" (192). Davies' work comes out of her experience in a military setting, and she notes that leadership can be isolating, lonely work, especially if a sole WPA's leadership model is considered anti-democratic or too authoritarian by people in their programs or by scholars in the field.

Authority is a heady construct limited by other local power structures. WPAs often don't have the opportunity to "wield power" (Phelps) and many in insecure positions may not wish to, as it could implicate responsibility for negative consequences. Regardless of position, though, "the WPA isn't exactly *free* to do what she believes is the right thing" (Leverenz 104). When agency is curtailed, Carrie S. Leverenz argues, "theorizing ethics is one way for WPAs to respond productively to what may seem an endless stream of irresolvable dilemmas" (106). These ethics may be communicated in a number of institutionally approved ways: Through organizational charts that clearly locate the director as program leader; through programmatic mission and position statements; through targeted professional development that addresses emerging concerns in the program (such as the bounds of free speech in our classrooms, to return to our opening narratives); or through the WPA's administrative philosophy that may be available to either those in the program or publicly.

The "philosophical job description," in particular, has been taken up in prior research as a genre primed for feminist inflection. E. Shelley Reid recommends that WPAs craft and share these types of documents to move their work beyond a strict focus on daily, mundane, and reactive tasks. Reid proposes a philosophical job description to ground her "all-terrain mentoring," which work together to provide a "multipurpose, good enough feminist administrative vehicle for the various kinds of caring, agency, and activism WPAs are capable of doing" (133). Further, WPAs would be well served to situate this philosophy within local institutional values. As Joseph Janangelo articulates, institutional mission is a "motor for action" that "connotes vision and purpose" and "ask[s] everyone to work together for a shared purpose" (xii). Identifying values shared between the institution and the writing program helps close the gap between WPAs' expected roles and their potential as visionary leaders. The writing program may thus connect its charge with larger goals, visibly demonstrating that writing instruction is a valuable part of the motor for action at the university. According to Jennifer Heinert and Cassandra Phillips, in order to enact systematic change, writing teachers—here, extended to include WPAs—must make their disciplinary expertise "both visible and valued" (128). Heinert and Phillips set a tall order. The value of a writing program, or of classes that teach required writing courses without a formal programmatic structure, remains bound in its perception as a service course. Philosophical job descriptions or administrative philosophies may articulate visionary goals and offer a way to front disciplinary expertise as a method of informed leadership. That is, the visibility of the WPA's ethical commitments (to goals like student success, retention, learning, and collaboration) and engagement in the discipline of writing studies can counterpoint more shallow concepts of what it means to head a writing program.

Situating one's feminist approaches in an ethically oriented theoretical frame allows WPAs to communicate their commitments, even if conditions prevent action. By situating their ethical goals within those of the institution, WPAs create a space where shared values are visible and clearly situate the writing program as a serious ethical endeavor.

Coalition Building Beyond Collaboration

As noted, distributed administrative models may seek to employ a feminist method in demonstrating a decentered location of power, but this decentering may come at a price. Likewise, collaboration can be risky, especially as so many WPAs work in insecure positions and because institutional values still often place "individual (or presented as such)" work above that of engaged groups (Heinert and Phillips 128). Heinert and Phillips recommend coalition building to supplement collaborative methods, as a coalition "has common goals, works purposely toward them, and shares credit and responsibility through the work" (129). A coalition is "collaboration in support of a strategic purpose" (Heinert and Phillips 128) and can work in tandem with feminist leadership models to create networks of caring, focused scholars committed to visionary change.

WPAs have many coalition partners across campus, disciplinary and otherwise. In the days immediately following the election, program administrators may have found themselves asking legal questions about the bounds of free speech; connecting students with campus resources like the Counseling Center, student legal aid, or the Women's Center; and interfacing with other units on campus responsible for student affairs. The philosophical job description could articulate these shared commitments among campus units, situating the writing program as one among many supportive resources on campus.

WPAs likely already do this important connective labor, if our meeting schedules are any indication. The shift in focus, I believe, is visibly reframing this work as interpersonal and interprofessional relationships based on a core set of ethical, feminist-informed considerations and focused on specific outcomes.

The Exhausted Visionary

But, truly, what practical use is a leadership vision if the WPA is too exhausted, too drawn in multiple directions, and too constrained by local power systems to enact it? Many WPAs experience the pressure of moving quickly from one project to another, feeling, as Laura Micciche so aptly describes, "physically and mentally overtaken by the enormity of the job"

(73). Under typical circumstances, the job of the WPA can feel like endless firefighting, and we understand our current circumstances to be atypical.

Micciche's slow agency grounds its approach in FemAdmin, emphasizing the relationship between agency and the drive for WPA efficiency. In their rush for an institutionally-approved resolution, WPAs may find themselves caught out, responsible for decision-making, yet often powerless against the institution's mandates. This approach "suggests that the speed of getting things done, along with the enormity of tasks involved, creates ideologies and practices that disrespect and dehumanize programs and people" (Micciche 79). In the days after the election, which soon stretched into weeks and now years, I found myself pushed to demonstrate the institution's practical values: efficiency, correctness, authority, objectivity, and promptness. The writing program and its faculty were abstractions I negotiated with other units on campus. Discussions about upholding mandates were about protecting the institution from bad publicity or legal scrutiny, not about Megan's devastating sexual assault and re-traumatization or Amy's anxiety about her unpredictable and aggressive student. Disrespect and dehumanization rightly describe these experiences from a program administrator's perspective.

Elaine Maimon's leadership narrative from WPA to college president contends with this maddening push for efficiency and its role in ethical decision-making. She describes the differences between "speed" and "haste" in leadership decisions as differences in readiness (12). Decisions made with speed move forward when the WPA (or any campus leader) has thoughtfully considered her options. Haste, on the other hand, moves decisions forward with incomplete understanding, and it often leads to regret.

Many WPA decisions must be made quickly, as deferring those actions can have negative consequences for those we serve. While speed cannot be avoided, Maimon argues, hastiness can. Vision is key to avoiding hasty decision making, with vision defined as "undeterred attention to mission and goals. But . . . it also requires peripheral vision" (11). Maimon articulates her leadership journey as one entangled with her identification as a woman. Her "double vision," of focus and periphery, emanates from anthropologist Mary Catherine Bateson's recognition of the demands placed on "women who spend years with one ear open for the cry of an awakened child, the knock of someone making a delivery, the smell of burning that warns that a soup left to simmer slowly has somehow boiled dry" (qtd. Maimon 11). Historically, women's life experiences have demanded they juggle macro and micro concerns; that is, women's lives "offer special preparation in keeping eyes on the prize, while simultaneously observing the process involved in winning the prize" (12). Biological essentialism notwithstanding, Maimon's point is well taken. Women in academic leadership positions are aware of their gender performance within the profession and its possible effects. These effects multiply intersectionally; race, class, sexual orientation, age, ability status, and other factors interact with gender to affect women's leadership access and experiences in academia. Importantly, Maimon acknowledges the intense emotional and cognitive demand placed on women in leadership positions who feel a deep responsibility for the well-being of those in their programs and who strive to frame their work as ethical sites of action. Vision and visibility become the concepts that emerge to thwart the institution's relentless push to efficiency. Exhaustion and top-down pressure are part of the WPA story, but so can be vision and visibility.

As I have argued, women-identified WPAs are especially situated to emerge as the leaders poised to effect change in their programs and more broadly. Louise Wetherbee Phelps recognizes composition's potential to dramatically influence undergraduate education. She envisions a future where first-year writing is not merely "tolerated and contained but becomes a positive force in higher education" (291). WPAs broker this change, as they step into new leadership roles and exert their rich experience.

I wish to conclude not with a proposal for what a feminist writing program leader might look like, act like, or do, understanding that many of us work under the radar for fear of professional consequences for ourselves or our faculty. Instead, I summarize and clarify some of the characteristics of feminist leadership discussed in the previous paragraphs. A feminist leadership model in writing program administration might:

- Take up program leadership as an ethical endeavor and make these ethics visible.
- Embrace power as a positive construct where the WPA practices careful and deliberate authority.
- Focus on coalition building instead of or in addition to collaboration.
- Work to refuse ideological purity, understanding the danger of rigid approaches to problem solving.
- Make commitments and values visible through visionary structures valued at the university, such as administrative philosophies and philosophical job descriptions, curricula, courses, professional development, and mission and position statements.
- Work to understand the differences between speed and haste, focusing on ethical decision making over efficiency.
- Practice intersectional administration that acknowledges the complex relationships individuals may have to the institution.

Phelps concludes her landmark piece, "Becoming a Warrior"—a metaphor from which many WPAs still draw strength—with this thought: "[E]thical conduct lies, at least for a time, in seriously trying" (317). Early scholarship on FemAdmin could not have anticipated the political crisis in which we find ourselves. Feminist writing program administration must now contend with the encroachment of real authoritarianism as vulnerable students and faculty express growing fears. We cannot halt many of the daily challenges we encounter as WPAs and as thoughtful, ethical citizens; however, we can build out from our positions to make our personal and programmatic commitments clear, even if those actions are incremental or quiet. It is incumbent on feminist writing program administrators to consider the ways in which they might be called to step into new leadership roles that demand ethical visions and visibility.

Notes

1. It bears noting that counter-protest merchandise, such as "Pink Pussy Hats" connected to the 2017 Women's March on Washington, D.C., were soon made available for purchase.

2. All identifying information has been changed. This project was cleared from IRB requirements as "not human subjects research," North Carolina State University, Sponsored Programs and Regulatory Compliance, IRB protocol number 12137. Both GTAs gave the author written permission to share their experiences in this format.

Works Cited

Bishop, Wendy. "Learning Our Own Ways to Situate Composition and Feminist Studies in the English Department." *JAC*, vol. 10, no. 2, 1990, pp. 339-55.

Cole, Kirsti, and Holly Hassel, editors. *Surviving Sexism in Academia: Strategies for Feminist Leadership*. Routledge, 2017.

Davies, Laura J. "Command and Collaboration: Leading as a New WPA." Adams Wooten, Babb, and Ray, pp. 188-203.

Dickson, Marcia. "Directing Without Power: Adventures in Constructing a Model of Feminist Writing Program Administration." *Writing Ourselves into the Story*, edited by Sheryl L. Fontaine and Susan Hunter, Southern Illinois UP, 1993, pp. 140-53.

Elder, Cristyn, and Bethany Davila, editors. *Defining, Locating, and Addressing Bullying in the WPA Workplace*. Utah State UP, 2019.

Fedukovich, Casie, and Sue Doe. "Beyond Management: The Potential for Writing Program Leadership During Turbulent Times." *Reflections: A Journal of Community Engagement, Writing, & Rhetoric*, vol. 18, no. 2, 2019, pp. 87-117.

Fine, Marlene G., and Patrice M. Buzzanell. "Walking the High Wire: Leadership Theorizing, Daily Acts, and Tensions." *Rethinking Organizational and Managerial Communication from Feminist Perspectives*, edited by Patrice M. Buzzanell, SAGE, 2000, pp. 128-56.

George, Diana, editor. *Kitchen Cooks, Plate Twirlers, & Troubadours: Writing Program Administrators Tell Their Stories*. Boynton/Cook, 1999.

Gladstein, Jill, and Brandon Fralix. *National Census of Writing*, 2013. Accessed 20 Sept. 2021.

Goodburn, Amy, and Carrie Shively Leverenz. "Feminist Writing Program Administration: Resisting the Bureaucrat Within." Jarratt and Worsham, pp. 276-90.

Heinert, Jennifer, and Cassandra Phillips. "From Feminized to Feminist Labor: Strategies for Creating Feminist Working Conditions in Composition." Cole and Hassel, pp. 127-35.

Hesford, Wendy. "'Ye Are Witnesses: Pedagogy and the Politics of Identity." Jarratt and Worsham, pp. 132-52.

Janangelo, Joseph, editor. *A Critical Look at Institutional Mission: A Guide for Writing Program Administrators*. Parlor Press, 2016.

Jarratt, Susan C., and Lynn Worsham, editors. *Feminism and Composition Studies: In Other Words*. Modern Language Association, 1998.

LaFrance, Michelle, and Elizabeth Wardle, editors. "Building a Twenty-First Century Feminist Ethos: Three Dialogues for WPAs." *WPA: Writing Program Administration*, vol. 42, no. 2, 2019, pp. 13-36.

Leverenz, Carrie S. "Theorizing Ethical Issues in Writing Program Administration." *The Writing Program Administrator as Theorist: Making Knowledge Work*, edited by Shirley K Rose and Irwin Weiser, Boynton/Cook, 2002, pp. 103-115.

Maimon, Elaine. *Leading Academic Change: Vision, Strategy, Transformation*. Stylus, 2018.

Mayfield, Jacqueline, Milton Mayfield, and William C. Sharbrough III. "Strategic Vision and Values in Top Leaders' Communications: Motivating Language at a Higher Level." *International Journal of Business Communications*, vol. 52, 2015, pp. 97-121.

McNaughtan, Jon, Hugo Garcia, Ian Lertora, Sarah Louis, Xinyang Li, Alexis L. Croffie, and Elisabeth D. McNaughtan. "Contentious Dialogue: University Presidential Response and the 2016 US Presidential Election." *Journal of Higher Education Policy and Management*, vol. 40, no. 6, 2018, pp. 533-49.

Micciche, Laura. "For Slow Agency." *WPA: Writing Program Administration*, vol. 35, no. 1, 2011, pp. 73-90.

Micciche, Laura, and Donna Strickland. "Feminist WPA Work: Beyond Oxymorons." *WPA: Writing Program Administration*, vol. 36, no. 2, 2013, pp. 169-76.

Miller, Hildy. "Postmasculinist Directions in Writing Program Administration." *WPA: Writing Program Administration*, vol. 20, nos. 1-2, 1996, pp. 49-61.

Phelps, Louise Wetherbee. "Becoming a Warrior: Lessons of the Feminist Workplace." *Feminine Principles and Women's Experience in American Composition and Rhetoric*, edited by Louise Wetherbee Phelps and Janet Emig, U of Pittsburgh P, 1995, pp. 289-340.

Ratcliffe, Krista, and Rebecca Rickly, editors. *Performing Feminist Administration in Rhetoric and Composition Studies*. Hampton Press, 2010.

Reid, E. Shelley. "Managed Care: All-Terrain Mentoring and the 'Good Enough' Feminist WPA." Ratcliffe and Rickly, pp. 128-41.

Rose, Shirley K, Lisa S. Mastrangelo, and Barbara E. L'Eplattenier. "Directing First-Year Writing: The New Limits of Authority." *College Composition and Communication*, vol. 65, no. 1, 2013, pp. 43-66.

Southern Poverty Law Center. "The Trump Effect: The Impact of the Presidential Campaign on Our Nation's Schools." Accessed 20 Sept. 2021.

Stenberg, Shari J. *Repurposing Composition: Feminist Interventions for a Neoliberal Age*. Utah State UP, 2015.

Strickland, Donna. *The Managerial Unconscious in the History of Composition Studies*. Southern Illinois UP, 2011.

Wooten, Courtney Adams, Jacob Babb, and Brian Ray, editors. *WPAs in Transition: Navigating Educational Leadership Positions*. Utah State UP, 2018.

Casie Fedukovich is Associate Professor of English and Director of the First-Year Writing Program at North Carolina State University. Her research on writing program administration, academic labor, and graduate teacher preparation appears in *Composition Studies*, *Composition Forum*, *Reflections: A Journal of Community-Engaged Writing & Rhetoric*, and *Workplace: A Journal for Academic Labor*.

Dedicating Time and Space for Women to Succeed in the Academy: A Case Analysis of a Women Faculty Writing Program at a Research 1 Institution

Kristin Messuri and Elizabeth A. Sharp

ABSTRACT

Using an institutionally sponsored women faculty writing program at a Carnegie Tier 1 research university as a site of analysis, the authors examine how sanctioned, dedicated time, space, and communities for writing affect participants' experiences of writing for publication. Drawing on the constant comparative method, we analyzed 206 surveys from women faculty participants over a three-year period. Findings indicated that the program was highly valued by participants because it offered a sanctioned, dedicated space for their research and increased participants' sense of belonging at the institution. The program also enhanced their writing practices and carved out a "safer" space for women in the male-centered academy.

WPAs and researchers are increasingly addressing the misconception that faculty have already developed effective writing skills and productive writing practices (Baldi et al., 2013; Geller & Eodice, 2013; Tulley, 2018). Even in writing studies, a field dedicated to the study and teaching of writing, there is little graduate-level writing instruction; instead, faculty typically learn to produce and publish scholarly writing on the job (Micciche & Carr, 2011; Wells & Söderlund, 2018). Although the need for faculty writing support has been identified in our field's literature, most institutions still lack programmatic writing support for faculty across all fields. Compounding the misconceptions that faculty are already skilled writers and do not need support, writing programs primarily serve student writers, a focus that is reflected in funding structures. Despite these challenges, writing programs and the institutions they are housed in should invest in faculty writers, whose career advancement depends on scholarly publication. In the context of writing programs, faculty-centered initiatives also have the potential to create rare institutional spaces where WPAs and faculty can engage in multidisciplinary dialogues that can influence the study and teaching of writing at postsecondary institutions (Clark-Oates & Cahill, 2013).

Existing faculty development typically centers on teaching rather than writing (Geller, 2013). The gap in faculty writing support is primarily being addressed by extra-institutional services such as the National Center for

Faculty Development and Diversity, writing advice published in periodicals and blogs such as *The Chronicle of Higher Education* and *Inside Higher Ed*, and academic self-help books (Belcher, 2009; Boice, 1990; Silvia, 2019; Sword, 2017). Many such efforts are spearheaded by current and former writing studies faculty and, therefore, are informed by our field's practices and research (Geller, 2013). However, by definition, external initiatives and resources cannot fully address local contexts. Institutionally sanctioned faculty writing initiatives exist in writing centers, teaching and learning centers, grant offices, and individual departments, but programmatic support is the exception rather than the rule. As institutional demands for research output increase, so too does the need for faculty writing support, particularly through sustained, pedagogically informed initiatives, which WPAs have the expertise to implement.

One response to the complex issues surrounding faculty writing efficacy and productivity is the development of institutionally embedded faculty writing groups. Writing groups of all forms are becoming increasingly popular means of promoting research writing in higher education (Aitchison & Guerin, 2014; Aitchison & Lee, 2006). Such groups vary widely in terms of goals, structures, activities, membership, and support offered (Haas, 2014). Common activities include self-directed or communal writing, other research-related activities such as reading research literature and working with data, providing feedback on ideas and writing projects, group discussions, and creating social connections with group members. There is a well-developed body of scholarship outlining benefits of writing groups: they have been found to increase participants' productivity (Fajt et al., 2013), serve as professional development sites (Garcia et al., 2013; Lee & Boud, 2003; Schick et al., 2011; Hunter et al., 2011; Smith et al., 2013), and provide social and emotional support (Badenhorst et al., 2013; Bosanquet et al., 2014; Cahir et al., 2014; Fajt et al., 2013; Lee & Boud, 2003). Faculty writing groups, in particular, may enhance members' teaching of writing (Smith et al., 2013) and, as previously noted, act as contact zones where WPAs can engage with faculty writers (Clark-Oates & Cahill, 2013).

Of the aforementioned studies, most were written by authors reflecting on their personal experiences. More voices are needed to better understand the variations of writing group members' experiences as well as how WPAs can effectively implement such groups in their home institutions. To extend the existing literature and respond to the need for faculty writing development, this article draws on survey data to explore an institutionally embedded writing program. Our site of analysis is a women faculty writing program at a Carnegie Tier 1 research institution. Throughout this article, we use the term "program" to encapsulate the scope of the groups' activities;

besides providing writing groups, the program offers writing retreats, networking events, and professional development opportunities exclusive to its participants. Another contribution of this study is analyzing a program of this size: it now serves nearly 100 faculty members who are placed in 11 groups that meet weekly throughout each semester.[1]

The program under study was created to promote equity for women faculty, who still face systemic barriers in the academy, including discrepancies in promotion and tenure, salaries, and recognition for their contributions (Crimmins, 2019; Geisler, 2010). COVID-19 has compounded such discrepancies (Malisch et al., 2020; Oleschuk, 2020). Mothers of young children, in particular, must negotiate intense demands on their time to succeed in the academy (Tulley, in press). Additionally, women faculty, compared to their male colleagues, traditionally allot less time to research, which is more highly valued in tenure and promotion processes, and more time to teaching (Modern Language Association, 2009) and service (Misra et al., 2011). Repercussions of deprioritizing research especially impact women associate professors, who "may hit a glass ceiling near the top of the ivory tower" due to disproportionate service commitments (Misra et al., 2011, para. 1). Writing initiatives have the potential to mitigate these structural inequalities, as they allow women faculty to dedicate time and space for their research (Grant & Knowles, 2000). Therefore, this program was created to promote structural conditions in which women faculty can prioritize research and writing as well as form a supportive community spanning academic ranks and departments.

Nearly all published discussions of writing groups document women-only writing groups, whether those gender dynamics occur by default or by design, as McGrail et al. (2006) found in their meta-analysis of research on faculty writing initiatives. Although their study is over a decade old, the focus on women's experiences has remained consistent. For many of these groups, the shared experience of navigating academia as women was central to its members' experiences of writing in a communal setting—and to the production of the very scholarship the group produced, as they co-authored articles on their group dynamics (Barry et al., 2004; Bosanquet et al., 2014; Fajt et al., 2013; Penney et al., 2015). Our study similarly reveals the centrality of gender to members' experiences, but on a larger scale compared to past studies, as we are unique in exploring a large, institutionally sanctioned, multidisciplinary program serving women faculty from all ranks.

Women Faculty Writing Program Background

To provide a women-only space that enhances women faculty's writing and research, the Women Faculty Writing Program (WFWP) was founded at Texas Tech University in 2015 by two faculty members and a writing center administrator (the co-authors and a colleague). The co-founders have backgrounds in Women's and Gender Studies and one had recently been engaged in a research project on women-only space, indicating powerful benefits of such space (Lewis et al., 2015) and, thus, were motivated to experiment with a women-only program. The program began during a time of growth and transition at the institution, which was designated a Carnegie Tier 1 institution that same year and a Hispanic-Serving Institution in 2017. WFWP's initial membership was 17 women faculty from four of the university's 12 colleges. Participants were provided space on campus, coffee, and a facilitator. Now in its fifth year, WFWP has nearly 100 members from all colleges.

Originally, the program was sponsored by the President's Gender Equity Council, the Writing Centers of Texas Tech University, and the Women's and Gender Studies Program, though we did not receive formal funding. We now receive funding, which pays for facilitators' stipends, writing retreats, food at networking events, and limited marketing materials. We felt we had a convincing argument for seeking funding after we kept better records of work done in the program, especially after we tracked details pertaining to grant proposals; the dollar amount, rather than the number of grant submissions, was the most compelling data point when requesting support from upper administration. In addition to the initial sponsors, WFWP now receives support (whether financial or in-kind) from the Office of the President; the Office of the Provost; the Office of Research and Innovation; the Division of Diversity, Equity, and Inclusion; and the Teaching, Learning, and Professional Development Center. Our growing collection of sponsors reveals the centrality of women's research to many university stakeholders and suggests the intricacies of administering such a program.

WFWP was modeled on the Indiana University (IU) Women Faculty Writing Groups (renamed the Faculty Writing Groups after they began to offer co-ed groups) developed by Laura Plummer. Like IU's groups, WFWP is divided into groups of about 9-15 writing "fellows" who meet for weekly writing sessions led by faculty facilitators. Each session begins with a half hour of goal setting and discussion revolving around a reading about productive writing or professional development, followed by two and a half hours of self-directed writing time. Unlike most writing groups described in past studies, in-meeting activities do not involve reading or responding to group members' writing. Instead, like the group described in Hixson et al. (2016), WFWP's structure emphasizes dedicated writing time and space, in keeping with our goals of promoting and sustaining a productive research writing culture for women faculty. The addition of structured, dedicated discussion and goal-setting time sets WFWP apart from writing groups documented in the literature.

Because the program was formed in response to disproportionate service loads placed on women faculty, facilitators strongly emphasize the need to protect this writing time, which members call "dedicated space" or "sacred time," where they commit to not only attending the entire meeting but also to eliminating distractions. Discussions emphasize regular, ongoing productive writing practices, but, given other demands on their time, this is the only scheduled, protected time some members have for writing in a given week. The program also responds to writers' needs for community-based support through feminist co-mentoring: mentoring relationships that emphasize nonhierarchical, relational learning and professional development (Bona et al., 1995). Providing space for formal networking and professional development is especially important for women faculty (Tulley, in press). As previous research has indicated, women faculty, in comparison to their male colleagues, continue to experience disadvantages with sanctioned networking and professional development both within their institutions and within their wider fields, including conferences and journals (Geisler, 2010).

As the program has grown in size, so too has it grown in complexity. Weekly writing sessions remain the bedrock, but the program has grown to further our goals of increasing research productivity, facilitating mentorship and collaboration, and creating a university-wide network of women scholars. Through a partnership with the Office of Research and Innovation, WFWP offers grant writing-focused groups, sometimes co-facilitated by members of that office who offer presentations and resources. WFWP fellows who identify as BIPOC can also opt into an affinity group, which we piloted after a conversation with Assata Zerai, then-Chief Diversity Officer at University of Illinois Urbana-Champaign, who led a group of Black women faculty. The group at our university, which members chose to name "Women Owning Writing," also operates as a means of enhancing equity for BIPOC women, for whom inequities experienced by women are exacerbated, including increased service loads and lower tenure and promotion rates (Gutiérrez y Muhs et al., 2012; Harley, 2008; Matthew, 2016). The "Women Owning Writing" group has collaboratively shared their experiences and provided guidance for establishing women faculty writing groups at the Faculty Women of Color in the Academy Conference (Alviña et al., 2019). Another unique group is a "drop-in" group initially developed for women administrators whose demanding schedules made the 15-week commitment untenable. The drop-in group runs in a similar manner as the other groups, but all members are permitted to participate, even if they only attend once or twice. Based on feedback from group members, increased childcare demands due to COVID-19, and evidence that mothers in the academy face unique conditions (Tulley, in press), we added a group for mothers with young children in the fall of 2020. (As of this writing, we have not collected survey data on this group.) Additionally, each year, WFWP holds a weekend writing retreat in a nearby town with the goal of making significant progress on a project. Other program activities have included networking events, write-ins (one-day community writing events), and speaking events where members share their expertise.

In providing women faculty with dedicated time, space, and community for writing, the program pursues the goals of creating a supportive, multidisciplinary network of women scholars that promotes mentorship and collaboration; enhancing research productivity and external funding; fostering productive, sustainable writing habits that serve members throughout their careers; facilitating interdisciplinary collaboration; and increasing rates of tenure and promotion among women faculty. Although writing productivity is not the only metric of success, documenting the number of writing projects submitted and accepted has increased institutional buy-in. Espousing the importance of intangible benefits of the program and, more importantly, substantiating those claims with quantifiable evidence of success has brought the program increased funding and visibility.

METHODS

Study Design

This study employed a data-driven methodology. Employing qualitative research methodologies beyond personal reflection provides compelling evidence for the efficacy of institutionally embedded writing groups to improve research productivity as well as the social and emotional well-being of women faculty participants.

At the end of each spring and fall semester from 2016 to 2018, a survey with open-ended questions was circulated among WFWP participants. The first author obtained IRB approval at our university.[2] Members participated voluntarily and were asked to answer questions about why they joined, their expectations for the program and for themselves, how (and if) the women-only aspect was relevant, their writing strengths and obstacles, and their productivity as measured in terms of projects submitted and accepted. We also asked about their demographic information. See the appendix for the survey. We modified questions slightly after the first semester and transitioned from administering the survey through an emailed Word document to administering the survey in person through paper forms plus emailed Word documents. These changes were implemented to garner richer responses and increase participation so that the data regarding participants' experiences would be more representative of the entire group. The response rate ranged from 24% to 66% over the six semesters data were collected. We collected 206 responses over the course of three years. Because many women remained in the group for multiple semesters, some individuals may have responded to the survey multiple times; however, their perceptions of WFWP and of themselves as writers may have shifted over time.

Analytical Process

The authors engaged in content analysis using the constant comparative method (Glaser, 1965). We closely analyzed responses, examining each idea and comparing each idea to previous ideas. If the idea was already mentioned, we grouped the idea with the similar idea. If an idea was not similar to previous ideas, we coded the idea as a new category. We reached saturation when no new ideas emerged (Roy et al., 2015). We then engaged in a more theoretical analysis, abstracting how the categories fit together and weaving the categories from the content analysis within the wider literature, guided by principles of constructivist grounded theory (Charmaz, 2006). As with all interpretative qualitative analyses, our perspectives inevitably influenced the analysis. Wherever possible, we used direct quotations, designating participants' words with quotation marks.

FINDINGS: BEING DEDICATED TO THE DEDICATED SPACE

Overwhelmingly, data indicated that participants highly valued and were committed to WFWP. They expressed a strong dedication to the program because it unapologetically carved out sanctioned time and space to think, write, and connect with other women. Specifically, the data revealed that the program's dedicated time and space allowed for: (a) developing and sharpening writing practices, (b) feeling an increased sense of belonging at the university, and (c) acknowledging and addressing the need for a women-only space within the male-centered academy.

Participants consistently indicated that the sanctioned three-hour block of writing time was crucial to their strong satisfaction with the program. Regularly designating time each week to research increased their research productivity. They claimed that WFWP was the only space they had that was "dedicated solely to research" during the week. Participants described the time set aside for the program as "reserved," "designated," "protected," "cherished," "secluded," and "focused," indicating a clear pattern of time scarcity for research. Participants often described the space as "sacred"—a "precious" time in their week.

Participants documented the need to schedule regular time for their research. One full professor explained why she joined the program: "I wanted the rigid time requirement of a regular meeting I must attend." Her need to schedule writing time as an obligation to engage in her research was a common thread and was especially the case for associate and full professors, who often had high service loads. An associate professor explained, "it is helpful for me to have time dedicated to my scholarly research that is scheduled away from distractions and obligations in my home department." The issue of avoiding distractions in the program was noted multiple times in the survey data—many faculty members indicated that they were unable to work in their offices because of interruptions from students or colleagues. In sharp relief from their office space, the WFWP space allowed them to "concentrate" on their writing.

Furthermore, the regular time set aside for writing helped participants structure their research goals beyond the three-hour meetings. One participant explained that the weekly meeting "centers my week and my research." Others scheduled additional writing times because they felt encouraged by their productivity in the WFWP meetings. Furthermore, the timing of meetings also impacted participants' writing productivity. One member discussed how the Friday afternoon meeting time "helped [her] move into the weekend feeling productive." This dedicated time helped participants focus on their writing projects; as one participant noted, WFWP "gave me precious time and peace of mind that I need to work." This participant perceived a relationship between "time" and "peace of mind" as central to her writing practices, emphasizing that WFWP both provided effective structural conditions and promoted emotional wellbeing.

Participants who are also administrators (approximately 1/3 of the sample) described an enhanced appreciation of the sanctioned time carved out weekly for their research. Administrators conveyed how little time outside of the writing program they had for research and, therefore, one used the word "precious" in describing the time afforded by WFWP. For one woman faculty administrator, "[T]his block of time is sometimes the only time I have to work on my research." Another appreciated the dedicated time WFWP provided, explaining, "by participating . . . I was guaranteed at least three hours of writing each week." Such responses are especially significant for administrators, as they generally have the highest service loads among faculty.

Beyond protecting research time from teaching and service, weekly meetings also helped participants negotiate domestic and family obligations, which are other structural barriers that can prevent women faculty research productivity (Baker, 2012). For example, an assistant professor with an infant and a toddler commented, "I can get a lot done in a little bit of time where I can devote my whole attention to a project and the group provided me time to focus." Responses about protecting time, especially from service and/or familial obligations, suggests that WFWP is one means to mitigate structural inequalities that affect women faculty.

Developing and Sharpening Writing Practices

Reserved time for writing was coupled with other factors that added to participants' high value assigned to the program. Participants consistently indicated they felt the structure helped them become more productive writers. Goal setting, readings, and discussions encouraged participants to regularly reflect on their writing practices and experiment with new strategies.

Being exposed to new writing strategies and integrating those strategies into their writing practices has increased many members' confidence and efficacy in their writing. As one participant stated, "The WFWP has given me confidence in my process of writing." Another woman described her added sense of competency:

> I feel much more competent with my writing, and I feel much more in control of the process. Rather than writing being something that happens due to external forces, I perceive greater say in when and how I write based on the strategies I have learned as part of this group.

Not all women commented that they were more confident in their writing. Often, these concerns had to do with structural issues in academia, in keeping with Tarabochia and Madden's (2018) findings that faculty writers are concerned about "time constraints that make scholarship feel rushed and disingenuous" (p. 435). For example, one participant noted, "I'm not feeling so positive about my writing, right now . . . I like to write, but slowly and thoughtfully and I don't have time for that if I want to be more productive." Even so, some responses suggested that the communal aspects of the program normalized writing concerns, which, in turn, increased participants' confidence in their writing. An associate professor noted that, in participating in WFWP, "you realize your struggles are not unique," further explaining that "its [sic] hard to leave the group not feeling energized and refreshed."

Feeling an Increased Sense of Belonging at the University

Another prominent thread in the data was the enhanced sense of connection with other women, and, by extension, a stronger sense of belonging at our university. No other space at our institution brings together faculty from divergent disciplines on a weekly basis—in fact, this program is one of the most sustainable multidisciplinary initiatives in place at our university. Moreover, our institution has no other program that consistently promotes the scholarship of such a large number of women.

Respondents identified the sense of belonging as a key reason they initially joined and continue to participate in the program. One member joined because she "Wanted to feel more at home," and others joined "to meet women faculty" and "build new relationships." Another noted that feelings of connectedness surpassed her expectations: "I think I did not expect to feel as connected as I did. I knew that I would experience some sense of camaraderie and community, but I did feel this much more strongly than I initially anticipated." Survey responses indicated that faculty who were new to the institution often joined WFWP with the explicit purpose of meeting new people, while existing members of the university expressed happiness at enhancing their network of colleagues.

In administering the program, we intentionally promote networks and connections by trying to place women at all ranks and women in as many disciplines as possible in each of the writing groups. We are committed to doing so to: (a) promote co-mentoring, (b) expose women faculty to other women's research across disciplines, and (c) encourage cross-fertilization of ideas and collaborations. Many participants indicated that the variety of ranks and disciplines were important reasons they valued the program. One participant explained, "I felt like the connections formed helped me network with more senior faculty members and helped make me feel a part of a larger community." Another stated, "I was eager to see how the group would evolve and gradually we came to know each other. I made new friends and colleagues with whom I will continue to work on some collaborative writing and research efforts." We consider these networks to be fundamental to the writing program's purpose.

Given this evidence that participation enhances members' sense of connection to the university, as administrators of this program, we make efforts to recruit incoming women faculty. Prior to their arrival, we send personal emails describing the program and inviting them to apply. We also participate in our university's new faculty orientation. Moreover, current members have used the program as a recruiting tool for new departmental hires.

Acknowledging the Need for Women-Only Space in the Male-Centered Academy

Participants' sense of belonging is connected to the women-only structure of the program. Another strong thread in the data was the acknowledgement of the need for women-only space in universities. In the survey, we asked, "How did the women-only aspect of the group affect your experience, if at all?" All but a few women indicated that the women-only component was critical—and a couple of members indicated that they would not have joined if the program were co-ed.

A prominent thread addressed safety. Women felt safe to express their concerns and experiences, felt "more at ease," and felt that they were not being judged. As one woman explained, "I'm not worried that I am being judged based on my gender and I feel like I can be more open about the struggle of being a woman in the academy." Other terms commonly employed to describe the significance of the women-only space included *safe, comfortable, open, supportive, encouraging*, and *non-competitive*. Many responses linked these qualities directly to the gendered nature of the groups. A participant explained, "It felt like it was a supportive environment due to the women-only aspect. It was nice to not have to qualify or apologize for discussions of work-life balance, confidence, or sharing personal information." Moreover, since the movements #MeToo in October 2017 and Time's Up in 2018, we noticed a trend in responses, with greater awareness of the need for women-only space during and after the fall of 2017. We discussed these findings in more depth in an invited talk focusing on feminist principles and feminist women-only space (Sharp & Messuri, 2017).

Additionally, Black Lives Matter and other movements engendered more discussion about racial injustice. WFWP carved out space for BIPOC women in a predominately white institution. Members of the "Women Owning Writing" group, who experience multiple dimensions of marginalization as BIPOC women, developed deeper connections with each other. One participant wrote that in this group, "there was the added ease of discussing the intersections of my identities and how these impact my work, scholarship, and productivity." Another stated, "For the women of color group, I feel like the expectation of feeling supported was greater. . . . these women knew me on a personal level—we shared real life stories and struggles and validated one another." This sense of validation further demonstrates the ability of faculty writing programs to provide crucial emotional and social support, especially for underrepresented faculty. In this sense, writing programs have the potential not only to mitigate structural conditions preventing women faculty's career advancement but also to enhance their sense of safety and connection in a male-dominated university. These benefits may be even more significant for those who experience multiple forms of oppression.

Discussion

The present study offers important contributions to the existing literature. This is one of the only known studies to examine a faculty writing program using a large number of surveys; moreover, these surveys were collected over a three-year period, capturing data as the program grew and its membership increased. The study responds to wider concerns regarding women faculty members' depleted time for research and the misperception that most faculty members can be highly productive scholars without writing support. Findings indicated that the Women Faculty Writing Program at our Carnegie Tier 1 research university was effective, valued, and needed. Women in our sample expressed commitment to the program because it offered regular, dedicated time and space for engaging in research, writing, and connecting. Women faculty of all ranks in WFWP needed consistent sanctioned time and space to concentrate on their research and to regularly engage with women faculty colleagues from departments across campus.

The voices of the writing group members included in this article overwhelmingly demonstrate the value of such programs as faculty writing support initiatives. For universities, the importance of offering an institutionally embedded faculty writing group cannot be understated. The women in our program indicated that the institutionally recognized, dedicated time and space had a variety of benefits, including improving research productivity, sharpening their writing skills, feeling more in control of research output, connecting with other women, and participating in a supportive space within the academy.

Although we understand members' development of productive writing practices to be the most significant outcome of this program, we recognize the significance of quantifiable results, both because research productivity is central to the career advancement of faculty and because such results justify the need for institutional support of such initiatives. We have found measurable indicators of program efficacy—especially counting the number of publications and the dollar amounts of grants funded—to be crucial to garnering institutional support and funding, especially from upper administration.

Limitations and Future Research Directions

This study provided a replicable, aggregable, data-driven methodology (Haswell, 2005) to explore writing group formation and efficacy for one women-only faculty writing program at a Carnegie Tier 1 university. As with all studies, there are limitations. The case study genre is necessarily limited, as unique conditions of this institutional setting, group dynamics, and experiences of individual participants affect writing group efficacy.

Survey-based methodologies also have limitations; the response rate ranged from 24% to 66% over the six semesters of data collection, so not all group members' views were collected. WFWP members who had low attendance, did not believe the program to be effective, or felt less of a sense of belonging may not have taken the survey or may have been absent when surveys were distributed. Some may have selected to leave the program or stop attending meetings. Surveys were distributed at the end of each semester, a notoriously busy time for faculty, which may have affected response rates. The mode of distribution changed from online (which had a lower return rate) to onsite distribution followed by an email containing the survey. Moreover, the methods employed in this study represent snapshots of participants' experiences; a longitudinal study is needed to explore how participants' writing practices and experiences with the program changed over time.

The women-only membership has proven effective for nearly all participants in this study, but, as McGrail et al. (2006) point out, most writing group research has studied women. This group structure may be transferable to other underrepresented groups with similar effects; in fact, the responses from the Women Owning Writing group reinforce this possibility. A few participants have suggested groups for LGBTQIA faculty. Such spaces may allow faculty from other traditionally underrepresented groups the same sort of supportive environment that WFWP members have identified. Moreover, co-ed groups following similar group structures and principles may also be effective, though the data largely indicated that members believed the women-only atmosphere was central to the program's supportive environment.

Presumably, the women faculty who elect to join and remain in WFWP are supportive of the program's principles and practices and, therefore, may find the structure more effective than a more general sample of women faculty or faculty of all genders. For example, WFWP members may be more open to women-only spaces, more interested in writing in communal environments, or more in need of structured time away from service. They may already value productive writing practices, as they elected to join a writing accountability group. This assumption is borne out by the thread in the data that identified writing productivity as a writing concern and/or strength. Since membership in the program, like participation in the survey, is self-selected, members' individual characteristics affect the generalizability of the results.

The institutional structure also affected members' experiences with the writing program, as we have shown. This program is effective for faculty in our specific institutional context. Writing programs that are not embedded in and supported by institutions likely function differently, as do programs in different types of institutions, especially those that emphasize research less. The multidisciplinary scope of the program, as well as the range of faculty positions included, also influenced group members' experiences. Cultural differences due to region/country may cause results to vary, as could gender or racial makeup of the institution. For example, writing programs may function differently in women-only colleges, in which women-only spaces proliferate.

Conclusion: Faculty Writing Programs in the Institution

Institutions of higher education, on the whole, continue to overlook the need to offer regular, sustained support for faculty writing and research. As this study suggests, institutions—and, more specifically, writing programs—would do well to dedicate space and resources to faculty writing programs, especially programs focusing on women and other minoritized faculty. The payoff for sanctioned faculty writing programs is significant. As the women in our sample expressed, tangible, regular institutional investment in their research through the writing program engendered a greater sense of belonging and collaborations, sharpened their writing practices, eand increased their productivity. Additionally, participants regularly engaged in both formal and informal discussions of writing, including teaching and writing in the disciplines, an outcome that aligns with the goals of many WPAs, thereby making writing programs natural institutional homes and partners for faculty writing programs. As a result of the faculty writing program, women demonstrated renewed dedication to their research and writing and to our institution.

Notes

1. Other large-scale faculty writing programs exist, notably Indiana University's Scholarly Writing program, whose Faculty Writing Groups were the inspiration and model for our program. However, large-scale programs are not documented in the literature.

2. RB 2016-5

References

Aitchison, Claire, & Guerin, Cally. (2014). Writing groups, pedagogy, theory and practice: An introduction. In Claire Aitchison & Cally Guerin (Eds.), *Writing groups for doctoral education and beyond: Innovations in practice and theory* (pp. 27–54). Routledge.

Aitchison, Claire, & Lee, Alison. (2006). Research writing: Problems and pedagogies. *Teaching in Higher Education, 11*(3), 265–278. https://doi.org/10.1080/13562510600680574

Alviña, Karina; Flores, Nadia; Lacerda, Carla; Lavender-Bratcher, Debra; Mendez-Morse, Sylvia; Piña-Watson, Brandy; & Shin, Sungwon. (2019, April 11–13). *Women owning writing* [Workshop]. 7th Annual Faculty Women of Color in the Academy Conference, Blacksburg, VA, United States.

Badenhorst, Cecile Marie; Penney, Sharon C.; Pickett, Sarah; Joy, Rhonda; Hesson, Jacqueline Barbara; Young, Gabrielle; McLeod, Heather; Vaandering, Dorothy; & Li, Xuemei. (2013). Writing relationships: Collaboration in a faculty writing group. *AISHE-J: The All Ireland Journal of Teaching and Learning in Higher Education, 5*(1), 1001–1026. https://ojs.aishe.org/index.php/aishe-j/article/view/100/152

Baker, Maureen. (2012). *Academic careers and the gender gap*. University of British Columbia Press.

Baldi, Brian; Sorcinelli, Mary Deane; & Yun, Jung H. (2013). The scholarly writing continuum: A new program model for teaching and faculty development. In Anne Ellen Geller & Michele Eodice (Eds.), *Working with faculty writers* (pp. 38–49). Utah State University Press.

Barry, Terri Trupiano; Bevins, Julie Galvin; Crawford, Maryann K.; Demers, Elizabeth; Hara, Jami Blaauw; Hughes, M. Rini; & Sherby, Mary Ann K. (2004). A group of our own: Women and writing groups: A reconsideration. In Beverly J. Moss, Nels P. Highberg, & Melissa Nicolas (Eds.), *Writing groups inside and outside the classroom* (pp. 378–414). Lawrence Erlbaum Associates.

Belcher, Wendy L. (2019). *Writing your journal article in 12 weeks: A guide to academic publishing success* (2nd ed.). University of Chicago Press.

Boice, Robert. (1990). *Professors as writers: A self-help guide to productive writing*. New Forums Press.

Bona, Mary Jo; Rinehart, Jane; & Volbrecht, Mary Rose. (1995). Show me how to do like you: Co-mentoring as feminist pedagogy. *Feminist Teacher, 9*(3): 116-124.

Bosanquet, Agnes; Cahir, Jayde; Huber, Elaine; Jacenyik-Trawöger, Christa; & McNeill, Margot. (2014). An intimate circle: Reflections on writing as women in higher education. In Claire Aitchison & Cally Guerin (Eds.), *Writing groups for doctoral education and beyond: Innovations in practice and theory* (pp. 374–398). Routledge.

Charmaz, Kathy. (2006). *Constructing grounded theory: A practical guide through qualitative analysis.* SAGE Publications.

Clark-Oates, Angela, & Cahill, Lisa. (2013). Faculty writing groups: Writing centers and third space collaborations. In Anne Ellen Geller & Michele Eodice (Eds.), *Working with faculty writers* (pp. 111–126). Utah State University Press.

Crimmins, Gail. (Ed.). (2019). *Strategies for resisting sexism in the academy: Higher education, gender and intersectionality.* Palgrave Macmillan.

Fajt, Virginia; Gelwick, Fran I.; Loureiro-Rodríguez, Verónica; Merton, Prudence; Moore, Georgianne; Moyna, María Irene; & Zarestky, Jill. (2013). Feedback and fellowship: Stories from a successful writing group. In Anne Ellen Geller & Michele Eodice (Eds.), *Working with faculty writers* (pp. 163–174). Utah State University Press.

Garcia, Elena Marie-Adkins; Eum, Seung hee; & Watt, Lorna. (2013). Experiencing the benefits of difference within multidisciplinary graduate writing groups. In Anne Ellen Geller & Michele Eodice (Eds.), *Working with faculty writers* (pp. 260–278). Utah State University Press.

Geisler, Cheryl. (2010). Gender equity in the Rhetoric Society of America. In Michelle Smith & Barbara Warnick (Eds.), *The responsibilities of rhetoric* (pp. 269–277). Waveland Press.

Geller, Anne Ellen. (2013). Introduction. In Anne Ellen Geller & Michele Eodice (Eds.), *Working with faculty writers* (pp. 1–18). Utah State University Press.

Geller, Anne Ellen, & Eodice, Michele. (Eds.). (2013). *Working with faculty writers.* Utah State University Press.

Grant, Barbara, & Knowles, Sally. (2000). Flights of imagination: Academic women be(com)ing writers. *International Journal for Academic Development, 5*(1), 6–19. https://doi.org/10.1080/136014400410060

Glaser, Barney G. (1965). The constant comparative method of qualitative analysis. *Social Problems, 12*(4), 436–445. https://doi.org/10.2307/798843

Gutiérrez y Muhs, Gabriella; Niemannn, Yolanda Flores; González, Carmen G.; & Harris, Angela P. (Eds.) (2012). *Presumed incompetent: The intersections of race and class for women in academia.* Utah State University Press.

Haas, Sarah. (2014). Pick-n-mix: A typology of writers' groups in use. In Claire Aitchison & Cally Guerin (Eds.), *Writing groups for doctoral education and beyond: Innovations in practice and theory* (pp. 78–111). Routledge.

Harley, Debra A. (2008). Maids of academe: African American women faculty at predominately white institutions. *Journal of African American Studies, 12*(1), 19–36. https://doi.org/10.1007/s12111-007-9030-5

Haswell, Richard H. (2005). NCTE/CCCC's recent war on scholarship. *Written Communication, 22*(2), 198–223. https://doi.org/10.1177/0741088305275367

Hixson, Cory; Lee, Walter; Hunter, Deirdre; Paretti, Marie; Matusovich, Holly; & McCord, Rachel. (2016). Understanding the structural and attitudinal elements that sustain a graduate student writing group in an engineering department. *WLN: A Journal of Writing Center Scholarship, 40*(5–6), 18–25. https://wlnjournal.org/archives/v40/40.5-6.pdf

Lee, Alison, & Boud, David. (2003). Writing groups, change and academic identity: Research development as local practice. *Studies in Higher Education, 28*(2), 187–200. https://doi.org/10.1080/0307507032000058109

Lewis, Ruth; Sharp, Elizabeth; Remnant, Jenni; & Redpath, Rhiannon. (2015). "Safe spaces": Experiences of feminist women-only space. *Sociological Research Online, 20*(4), 9. https://doi.org/10.5153/sro.3781

Malisch, Jessica. L.; Harris, Breanna N.; Sherrer, Shanen M.; Lewis, Kristy A.; Shepherd, Stephanie L.; McCarthy, Pumtiwitt C.; Spott, Jessica L.; Karam, Elizabeth, P.; Moustaid Moussa, Naima; Calarco, Jessica McCrory; Ramalingam, Latha; Talley, Amelia E.; Cañas-Carrell, Jaclyn E.; Ardon-Dryer, Karin; Weiser, Dana A.; Bernal, Ximena E.; & Deitloff, Jennifer. (2020). Opinion: In the wake of COVID-19, academia needs new solutions to ensure gender equity. *Proceedings of the National Academy of Sciences, 117*(27), 15378–15381. https://doi.org/10.1073/pnas.2010636117

Matthew, Patricia A. (Ed.) (2016). *Written/unwritten: Diversity and the hidden truths of tenure.* The University of North Carolina Press.

McGrail, Matthew R.; Rickard, Claire M.; & Jones, Rebecca. (2006). Publish or perish: A systematic review of interventions to increase academic publication rates. *Higher Education Research & Development, 25*(1), 19–35. https://doi.org/10.1080/07294360500453053

Micciche, Laura R., & Carr, Allison D. (2011). Toward graduate-level writing instruction. *College Composition and Communication, 62*(3), 477–501.

Misra, Joya; Lundquist, Jennifer Hickes; Holmes, Elissa; & Agiomavritis, Stephanie. (2011, January–February). The ivory ceiling of service work. *Academe.* https://www.aaup.org/article/ivory-ceiling-service-work#.XiCjachKg2w

Modern Language Association. (2009, April 27). Standing still: The associate professor survey; Report of the Committee on the Status of Women in the Profession. https://www.mla.org/content/download/3120/80834/cswp_final042909.pdf

Oleschuk, Merin. (2020). Gender equity considerations for tenure and promotion during COVID-19. *Canadian Review of Sociology, 57*(3), 502–515. https://doi.org/10.1111/cars.12295

Penney, Sharon; Young, Gabrielle; Badenhorst, Cecile; Goodnough, Karen; Hesson, Jacqueline; Joy, Rhonda; McLeod, Heather; Pickett, Sarah; Stordy, Mary; Vaandering, Dorothy; & Pelech, Sharon. (2015). Faculty writing groups: A support for women balancing family and career on the academic tightrope. *Canadian Journal of Higher Education, 45*(4), 457–479. https://doi.org/10.47678/cjhe.v45i4.184396

Roy, Kevin; Zvonkovic, Anisa; Goldberg, Abbie; Sharp, Elizabeth; & LaRossa, Ralph. (2015). Sampling richness and qualitative integrity: Challenges for research with families. *Journal of Marriage and Family, 77*(1), 243–260. https://doi.org/10.1111/jomf.12147

Schick, Kurt; Hunter, Cindy; Gray, Lincoln; Poe, Nancy; & Santos, Karen. (2011). Writing in action: Scholarly writing groups as faculty development. *Journal on Centers for Teaching and Learning, 3,* 43–63.

Sharp, Elizabeth A., & Messuri, Kristin. (2017, November 30). Women-only writing space: Disrupting and enhancing the academy. [Invited keynote presentation.] Smith College, Northampton, MA, United States.

Silvia, Paul J. (2019). *How to write a lot: A practical guide to productive academic writing* (2nd ed.). American Psychological Association.

Smith, Trixie G.; Molloy, Janice C.; Kassens-Noor, Eva; Li, Wen; & Colunga-Garcia, Manuel. (2013). Developing a heuristic for multidisciplinary faculty writing groups: A case study. In Anne Ellen Geller & Michele Eodice (Eds.), *Working with faculty writers* (pp. 38–49). Utah State University Press.

Sword, Helen. (2017). *Air and light and time and space: How successful academics write.* Harvard University Press.

Tarabochia, Sandra, & Madden, Shannon. (2018). In transition: Researching the writing development of doctoral students and faculty. *Writing and Pedagogy, 10*(3), 423–452. https://doi.org/10.1558/wap.34576

Tulley, Christine E. (in press). *Rhet comp moms: Parenting, professionalism, and productivity.* Utah State University Press.

Tulley, Christine E. (2018). *How writing faculty write: Strategies for process, product, and productivity.* Utah State University Press.

Wells, Jaclyn M., & Söderlund, Lars. (2018). Preparing graduate students for academic publishing: Results from a study of published rhetoric and composition scholars. *Pedagogy, 18*(1), 131–156. https://doi.org/10.1215/15314200-4216994

Authors' Note Regarding the Recent Call to Boycott the Council of Writing Program Administrators

This piece was accepted for publication in *WPA: Writing Program Administration* in November 2020, prior to the recent call to boycott the Council of Writing Program Administrators (CWPA). After careful consideration and conversations with the editorial team, we, the authors of this piece, have decided to move forward with publishing in this journal, given the editorial team's action plan to reevaluate the journal's editorial practices as well as their description of relative autonomy from the CWPA. We stand in solidarity with those boycotting the CWPA and join their call for the organization to make meaningful structural changes that work to dismantle its culture of racism and white supremacy. We publish this piece in the hopes of advocating for needed support for faculty who have long been unrecognized and underrepresented, and we will not submit future work to WPA unless recommended changes have been made.

Kristin Messuri is Managing Director of the Writing Centers and co-founder and co-director of the Women Faculty Writing Program at Texas Tech University. Her research explores affect and writing initiatives. Recent scholarship includes projects examining the workings and efficacy of graduate and faculty writing communities and exploring the intersections of writing center work and disciplinary writing for graduate writing consultants.

Elizabeth A. Sharp is Director of Women's and Gender Studies, co-founder and co-director of the Women Faculty Writing Program, and Professor of Human Development and Family Sciences at Texas Tech University. Her research focuses on ideologies of gender, families, and relationships. Her recent projects have focused on bridal and wifely femininities and she engaged in a multi-year transdisciplinary research project integrating social science and dance.

Appendix

Survey

This survey is intended to gather information about your experiences in the Women Faculty Writing Program (WFWP), as well as your feelings about and experiences with writing in general. Your responses will be used for research purposes. Additionally, these questions are intended to help you to reflect on your writing practices. Participation is voluntary; you may skip any questions you do not wish to answer, and you may choose not to complete the survey.

Demographic Questions

1. Department:
2. Faculty rank:
3. Administrative duties, if any:
4. Gender:

Survey Questions

1. Why did you choose to join WFWP this semester? If this is not your first semester in WFWP, why did you choose to participate again?

2. How did the women-only aspect of the group affect your experience, if at all?

3. Throughout the semester, what **expectations** did you have (1) **for the group** and (2) **for yourself as a member of the group**?

4. How did your **experience** of the (1) **group dynamics** and (2) **as a member of the group** compare to those expectations?

5. What concerns or struggles with writing do you experience? What effect, if any, did participation in this group have on those concerns or struggles?

6. What are the positive aspects of your writing? What effect, if any, did participation in this group have on those strengths?

7. How did you spend your writing time during group meetings? Please consider both the tasks you completed (e.g., coding data, outlining, drafting, reorganizing) and the type of projects you worked on (e.g., article, chapter, monograph, conference paper, poster).

8. How many writing projects did you complete in the past **calendar year**? Provide the number and type (e.g., article, chapter, monograph, conference paper, poster).

9. How many writing projects did you complete in the past **semester**? Provide the number and type (e.g., article, chapter, monograph, conference paper, poster).

How Can We Better Support Teaching Multimodal Composition? A National Survey of Institutional Professional Development Efforts

Chen Chen

ABSTRACT

With the "multimodal turn" in the field of rhetoric and composition and the updated CWPA Outcomes Statement, writing studies scholars and teachers have come to define writing more broadly than as traditional alphabetic texts. But at the local institutional level, how have we been supporting writing instructors on teaching multimodality? In 2005, a group of scholars (Anderson et al.) sought to survey how multimodality was integrated into the writing curricula across the country. More than ten years later, I built off of that survey to give a snapshot of the current state of the field of institutional professional development efforts across the nation. I offer updated results to illustrate that there are still disparate beliefs on how big a role multimodality should play in writing classes, and that instructors do not receive adequate and/or effective formal professional training on teaching multimodality. Based on these results, I offer a framework for writing program administrators to approach professional development initiatives that combine theories and practices and take advantage of social learning models and resource sharing, with a consideration of their implications on labor issues.

INTRODUCTION

Ever since scholars in The New London Group introduced the "multimodal turn" (Kress; Kress and van Leeuwen; Arola, Ball, and Sheppard), multimodal composition has attracted much scholarly attention in the field of rhetoric and composition, and specifically in its subfield, computers and composition (Selfe; Selfe and Hawisher; Arola, Sheppard, and Ball). Many writing studies scholars have argued for the importance of expanding the understanding of what "writing" is beyond the traditional alphabetic text (Takayoshi and Selfe; Shipka; Wysocki, Johnson-Eilola, Selfe, and Sirc; Yancey). The need to include this dimension of writing was reflected in the revision of the Outcomes Statement for First-Year Composition in 2014 by the CWPA:

> In this Statement "composing" refers broadly to complex writing processes that are increasingly reliant on the use of digital technologies. Writers also attend to elements of design, incorporating images and graphical elements into texts intended for screens as well as printed pages. Writers' composing activities have always been shaped by the technologies available to them, and digital technologies are changing writers' relationships to their texts and audiences in evolving ways.

Writing pedagogy that addresses this extended definition of composing is driven by the need to prepare students for the kinds of communication that they have been and will be exposed to and practice in their personal, academic, professional, and civic life (Clark; Yancey). These arguments call for revisions of our writing curricula and pedagogical practices in response to "new models of writing" that have emerged in the twenty-first century and "to help our students compose often, compose well, and through these composings, become the citizen writers of our country, the citizen writers of our world, and the writers of our future" (Yancey 1).

Consequently, numerous professional development (PD) efforts have been undertaken at different levels to provide support and training to writing teachers on teaching multimodal composition and teaching writing with technology. As shown in the 2015 special issue of *Computers and Composition Online*, the impact of CIWIC (Computers in Writing-Intensive Classrooms, a two-week workshop run by Cindy Selfe at Michigan Tech University) and now DMAC (Digital Media and Composition, now a week-long workshop at The Ohio State University) has been significant on their participants and like ripples in a pond, to their students and colleagues at their own institutions. Such professional development efforts are groundbreaking in the field and continue to benefit many writing teachers and programs. However, material conditions often constrain diverse faculty participation. For example, many first-year writing courses are taught by contingent faculty who may not have the financial means to attend such costly workshops. Ultimately, these national-level professional development efforts represent a limited scope that can have difficulty reaching a broad audience.

In 2005, Dan Anderson, Anthony Atkins, Cheryl Ball, Krista Homicz Millar, Cynthia Selfe and Richard Selfe sought to investigate how multimodal composition was integrated into composition curricula by using a national survey in order to provide a "state-of-the-field" kind of snapshot. One of the sections in the survey focused on professional development efforts, aiming to discover "how teachers were preparing themselves to design and assess these assignments, how they were motivated and recognized for such work within institutional contexts" (Anderson et al. 60).

They found that instructors lacked "comprehensive, cohesive or effective" professional development support at their institutions and that often the support offered emphasized more learning how to use technologies rather than critical engagement and reflections with pedagogical practices such as assignment design and assessment when teaching multimodality (79). In 2015, a decade later, when reflecting on their experiences at CIWIC and DMAC, Rick Hunter, Alanna Frost, Moe Folk, and Les Loncharich still pointed out that local institutional professional development support often showed what Dickie Selfe refers to as an "inoculation approach" (cited in Hunter, Frost, Folk, and Loncharich).

More than ten years have passed since Anderson et al.'s comprehensive survey was conducted. The landscape of digital technologies has drastically changed, but the need for teaching multimodal composition has remained if not increased. Do the widespread use of digital technologies and the long scholarly legacy of multimodal composition mean that writing teachers are less resistant to teaching multimodality and that they need less support in doing so because they are more technologically savvy? What kinds of professional development efforts are now in place to support the teaching of multimodality? With this curiosity in mind, I built on Anderson et al.'s survey, especially the sections on definition of multimodality, teaching resources, pedagogical and technological training, and the assessment of technology training in order to investigate the research questions below:

- How have the attitudes toward teaching multimodality in writing programs changed since 2005 across the nation?
- How have writing instructors developed experiences and skills in teaching multimodality? What resources do they use to enhance their multimodality pedagogy? (In particular, I'm interested to see if instructors still rely more on their peers and self–teaching as concluded in the old survey.)
- What are the professional development opportunities offered by their programs, departments, and institutions?
- How is the labor of professional development in this area recognized by programs, departments, and institutions?

I hope the answers to these questions can provide us a glimpse of the current state of the field and prompt us to think of meaningful ways to develop sustainable professional development efforts in teaching multimodality that consider the material constraints and labor conditions of composition teachers.

Survey Design and Distribution

In an elaborate rationale, Anderson et al. argue for using a survey as "an act of definition" to "define multimodal compositions and their place within Composition Studies and English departments" (63). My survey is designed with a similar justification: to define attitudes toward teaching multimodality and PD efforts to support such teaching at the institutional level. I used a convenience sampling method through an open call that solicited participants on the WPA-L listserv as well as a call to writing program directors at institutions who participated in the 2005 survey, including both first-year writing and advanced writing programs. Seventy-nine participants started the survey, and forty-four completed the survey. The choice of convenience sampling was made for two reasons: (a) soliciting with an open call without identifying individual participants allowed the researcher to reach participants who might not be teaching in a program engaged in teaching multimodality, therefore leading to a more accurate state of multimodality teaching in writing curricula, and (b) reaching out to institutions that had participated in the 2005 survey can potentially present comparable results between the two surveys. As a result, respondents to the survey represent a diverse sample, coming from a variety of institutions, ranging from four-year research universities to liberal arts colleges to technical colleges.

My survey questions include four sections: multimodality in the writing program; teaching resources; training and professional development; individual and program demographics. In order to address the first research question, I want to gain a basic understanding of how multimodality is implemented in writing programs by asking questions about how it is defined at different programmatic levels and how individual instructors prioritize teaching multimodality in relation to any programmatic mandates or attitudes. In the second section, I sought to understand what kinds of teaching materials instructors use, such as textbooks, and where they obtain these resources as well as how they evaluate and what their needs are for current instructional materials. The third section is the main focus of the survey, asking questions about what kinds of training or PD support instructors receive and where they received it, as well as how their participation in such PD efforts is recognized and compensated. The last section provides an overview of the demographics of respondents and their programs.

It is important to note that while the old survey adopted a definition of multimodal composition performed with mostly digital tools and professional training on using technologies, the current survey extends the meaning of multimodal composition to include composing in modes that are not necessarily digital. Jody Shipka, in *Toward a Composition Made Whole*, cautions us that the emphasis on "new" technologies can lead to the tendency to equate multimodal composition with composing computer–based digitized, screen–mediated texts (8). She thus argues for the importance of broadening the meaning of "technology" to include, for example, three–dimensional objects. Therefore, my survey questions adopt a broad understanding of multimodality, and instead of just asking about how teachers are trained to use technologies (hardware and software), I ask about the training of teaching multimodal composition in general. Further, I aim to discover how PD efforts address both theoretical issues about multimodal pedagogy and practical teaching applications.

Results and Analysis

Demographic and Institutional Context of Survey Respondents

My survey respondents reflect an evenly distributed range of academic positions, from graduate students, to tenure-track professors, to two-year college instructors, full-time lecturers, and part-time lecturers, as well as academic specialists; no one category has more than 9 responses out of a total of 43 participants who answered that question. Compared with the 2005 survey, there are also more respondents who are teaching at a four-year institution with no graduate program in their department (n=11 instead of n=2). Thus, my survey results may reflect more accurately the state of professional training on teaching multimodal literacies at the undergraduate level. Respondents also show all levels of experiences in teaching multimodal composition—from never having taught it to having taught it for more than sixteen years—while the 2005 survey did not have any respondents who had never taught or taught multimodal composition for a year or less.

With this demographic information in mind, in the following sections, I will summarize and analyze the significant findings from the survey in response to my research questions as well as in comparison with the 2005 survey.

Teaching Multimodal Composition as an Individual Endeavor

One significant change in the survey results compared to 2005 is that the attitudes toward the integration of teaching multimodality into writing curricula have changed. It is clear that more people are holding teaching multimodal composition at a higher priority in their writing classes. When asked about what priority teaching multimodality holds for them, many fewer people put teaching multimodality as low or no priority than ten years ago. The old survey shows that 83% (n=34) of the respondents held it as low priority and 27% (n=11) as no priority whereas the new data show

8% (n=4) and 4% (n=2) respectively. At the same time, more than 90% of respondents (n=45) indicate that they would participate in teaching multimodal literacies, albeit in different ways.

Similarly, how multimodality is defined in writing programs has also changed. In the current survey, fewer respondents say that multimodality is defined as texts that are designed with attention to several/many modes of communication (29%, n=15) while more choose to define it as texts that are designed using a combination of words, images, animations, video, audio, physical objects, etc. (46%, n=24). Such responses may indicate that writing teachers now treat teaching multimodal composition both as an analytical and a productive endeavor. More teachers now may be paying attention to the different production elements that students ought to be engaged with in multimodal projects.

While the general attitude toward teaching multimodality seems to be more enthusiastic now, how it is taught specifically in classrooms is not always consistent and is very much up to individual writing instructors. When asked at what level the implementation of multimodal literacies happens, many still responded that it happens on an individual teacher basis (81%, n=42) and on a course basis (33%, n=17), reflecting similar results from the 2005 survey. However, respondents' perceptions of multimodal composition in writing classrooms do reflect an in-depth, rhetorical awareness of their pedagogical practices. It is also important to note that when cross tabulated with the demographic data, these various beliefs on how multimodality should be integrated into writing curricula are reflected across different kinds of institutions and programs where respondents work, whether four-year institutions or community colleges.

When asked to elaborate what role non-textual composition should play in the writing classroom (Q16), a variety of answers emerged that fall under these following categories:

- It should be integral in the writing class because it prepares students to write different genres in different kinds of contexts in the future. A typical response is: "Significant! It's important that students critically, rhetorically, and ethicality understand and communicate through/in multiple modes. It's also important that they learn to engage in meaning making processes by layering multiple modes."
- It should be integral in the writing class and it does not displace conventional alphabetic writing, because it helps students to learn the same kinds of rhetorical concepts and practice process work. A typical response is: "I think the majority of creation in the writing classroom should be multimodal. This doesn't displace writing itself, or

any of the more traditional goals of the writing classroom. Those skills are used in invention, documentation, and process work. But these conventions also must be 'translated' for multimodality, as the majority of writing that takes place in the workplace and in academia, I would argue, is multimodal (oral, digital, and written)."

- It should play some role, but it depends on the discipline and the purpose of the course, or as long as it fulfills the program's/course's learning outcomes and objectives. Some sample responses:
    - "I believe every student should have classroom experience with multimodal composition, but I do not think every course should be required to cover it. Basic writing skills must not be neglected, but neither should multimodal writing."
    - "A minor role in composition generally. In Writing in the Discipline courses, students should learn the discipline–specific use of graphical information."
    - "I think this depends widely on the discipline. In a composition class that serves all majors, I think more alphabetical text serves the largest number of students whose employers will likely judge them based on alphabetical texts and expect them to have mastered alphabetical texts before acquiring digital/multimodal authoring techniques."

Unfortunately, not all responses reflect an optimistic prospect for the development of multimodal curricula. A few respondents still see non-textual based, non-alphabetic writing as the main focus of their writing classes, where other modes of writing should either play a supplementing role or no role at all. Without further investigation into their curricula, it is unclear how much this perception is constrained by programmatic structures or policies or other material constraints. Perhaps multimodality will always be implemented at varying levels across institutions given the differing local and institutional contexts. However, conflicting perceptions can exist within the same institutional context, as one respondent pointed out that some faculty in their department "insist on assigning print-based compositions only." Such inconsistent perspective within one program or department can potentially create challenges for professional development efforts.

Often, instructors have a lot of freedom over what they can teach in their classes; without programmatic mandates on implementing multimodal composition, for example, individual instructors' attitudes toward multimodality can result in very different student learning experiences. At the same time, without programmatic structures, teaching materials on multimodality can also vary significantly, often leaving the responsibility of finding and developing instructional materials solely on individual instructors.

Compiling and Selecting Teaching Resources and Materials

If implementation of multimodality varies from classroom to classroom, the choices of teaching materials and textbooks also reflect similarly a level of individual freedom in teaching multimodality. Specifically, I asked a new question on who selects the textbook they use. While 36% (n=17) responded that they choose their own texts, 38% (n=18) indicated that the WPA or the writing program council selects the books. Only in two cases was a book voted on by all the instructors in the program. Even though new textbooks on teaching multimodality have been published since the old survey was administered, such as *Writer/Designer: A Guide to Making Multimodal Projects* and *Understanding Rhetoric*, many respondents (47%, n=16) still don't rely on textbooks to teach multimodality, visual rhetoric, or new media. Others also mention using parts of general composition textbooks such as *Everything's an Argument*, *Bedford/St. Martin's Guide to Writing*, *The Bedford Book of Genres*, and *The Academic Writer*, which, while not focused exclusively on multimodality, have some sections on multimodal composition. Among the use of textbooks, *Writer/Designer* is the most popular. In comparison, before this book was published, respondents in the 2005 survey often cobbled together more texts to teach multimodality. As a field, we may deduce that new textbooks on multimodal composition have provided useful resources that were long needed. Nonetheless, the more that teaching materials offer, the more writing instructors may be craving more resources and support for teaching multimodality.

Similarly, respondents expressed desires for textbook materials to cover more content that includes both analytical and production-oriented materials, such as:

- Media artifacts for study (e.g., images, audio, and video)
- Analytical exercises (e.g., texts with prompts for guided readings)
- Writing activities (e.g., response fields for freewriting or notetaking)
- Skills instruction (e.g., tutorials for using applications)
- Activities instruction (e.g., tutorials for conducting research, collaborating, or composing)

Many more respondents in the current survey also chose to offer other suggestions not listed in the options. These include a range of topics such as rhetorical strategies, design principles, cultural/social connections of technologies, and prompts and samples of productions. While most respondents in the 2005 survey said that instructional materials were missing content on rhetoric involving animations and motions (77%, n=30), most of my survey respondents point out the lack of coverage of cultural dimensions of new media (76%, n=29). These results may not be surprising given the development of digital technologies over the past decade and the field of computers and composition, which reflect a disciplinary trend toward more emphasis on critical and rhetorical literacies in researching and teaching about composing with new media that attune to the social and cultural perspectives on media consumption and production.

Efforts on Training and Professional Development

Not only do individual instructors take on the responsibilities of selecting and compiling materials for teaching multimodality, they also rely heavily on their own professional and social networks to support their pedagogical endeavors, more so than structured and/or required institutional and programmatic professional development training efforts. Compared to the 2005 survey, although there is an increasing percentage of participants who take advantage of the departmental and institutional workshops, the large majority of instructors still rely on self-training. In order to find out more whether instructors have received training on teaching multimodality and where they've received it, I added these questions in the new survey. Slightly more than half of the respondents who answered the question (57%, n=25) said that they have been trained to teach multimodality. When asked where they received such training, the majority said they received it from either graduate school education (67%) or informal mentoring by other instructors/faculty (37%). A third of respondents also indicated that they learned much through their own trainings or professional networks outside their institutions such as DMAC and the computers and writing community. Only 10% said they received it from program and institutional workshops.

In response to questions about professional development support for different areas, a large majority of instructors (around 90%) responded that they rely on self-training when it comes to learning and assessing new software and systems as well as planning and integrating multimodal assignments into their classes. However, compared with the 2005 survey, more people chose departmental and institutional workshops, and fewer people selected workshops offered at other institutions or other social networks such as listservs or colleagues at other institutions. This may be a positive sign, indicating that programs, departments, and institutions may value multimodal composition more by providing more professional development opportunities to support writing teachers teaching multimodality. Nonetheless, when asked about how other teachers in their program/department receive support in these areas, we begin to see some problems with institutional professional development efforts or the lack thereof. The answers in the comment box here show more explicitly that many instructors still need to be more proactive and rely on self-training when it comes to getting help, as exemplified in these responses:

- "When it comes to my institution's resources, training and workshop options, IT knowledge, individualized Helpdesk help, there is much to be desired."
- "Some teachers are very engaged with departmental seminars. Others are more self-taught. Overall, though, I think people do it like me: by trying out recommendations from friends and colleagues."
- "Faculty at my institution have to be proactive if they want to incorporate multimodal literacies. It is very much an individual instructor's choice."

In order to investigate programmatic and institutional structures for PD efforts, my survey focused on asking questions about any required workshops for training to teach multimodality. Most of the responses showed that such workshops are not really required and that attendance is low. However, it is gratifying to see that around 40% of respondents indicated that workshops on implementing multimodality in classrooms take various forms: tool-oriented: focused on learning the technology; presentation based: presenter sharing their own assignments; hands-on: making your own multimodal assignments; discussion-based: talking about challenges and issues related to teaching multimodality.

On the one hand, for all institutions who offer these workshops, the pedagogical/theoretical issues covered in this training include a wide range: theories and practices of multimodal literacies; assessment of multimodal assignments; student/user agency with technology; rhetorical analysis of technologies within classroom settings. On the other hand, the nature of learning in these workshops varies depending on the types of institutions (see Table 1). The majority of the responses indicate that these workshops, if required, are often offered once a semester. Even when these workshops were offered, very few respondents found them very effective (5%, n=2), just as very few people found the technology training to be very effective in the 2005 survey. Further, very few places offer assessment on teaching multimodality at the program level, and university level assessment of such PD efforts is rarely done. Suggestions on how to improve this training show that there is still a high demand for more time/opportunities to experiment with teaching/learning in digital environments, including more time and opportunities to either gain more knowledge of technology or to integrate multimodality in the classroom.

Table 1

Cross-Tabulated Data of Program Information with the Nature of Learning in Required Multimodality Workshops.

		Four-year college/ university with a PhD program	Four-year college/ university with no graduate program	Community college
What is the nature of learning in the multimodal literacies implementation workshops?	Tool oriented: focused on learning the technology	9	2	4
	Presentation based: presenter sharing their own assignments	7	5	2
	Hands-on practice of making your own multimodal assignments	5	4	4
	Discussion-based: talking about challenges and issues related to teaching multimodality	9	4	3

It is interesting to see through cross tabulation the kinds of institutions that are more likely to offer these workshops, the content of these workshops, and how well they are attended. While overall a majority of the institutions represented by respondents of the survey do not offer required workshops, four-year colleges or universities with a PhD program are more likely to offer them. When offered, these workshops are led by a variety of instructors, from graduate students to contract/adjunct faculty to tenured/tenure-track faculty and to university assigned instructors, and they are often offered in the English department or some kind of institutional-wide faculty technology support center. What's at stake here is also the issue of labor conditions and power dynamics among these different types of writing teachers. Given that most instructors teaching writing courses, especially in the Gen Ed curricula, are likely contingent faculty, it's unethical to simply require such participation in professional development activities when they are in precarious positions if such participation "is not at least indirectly rewarded or evaluated" (Lalicker and Lynch-Biniek 96).

I thus wanted to find out how such labor was being perceived at the institutional level: is this labor recognized, acknowledged, and/or rewarded? Most respondents said that instructors got no reward for teaching multimodality. However, the 2005 survey showed that there were some rewards offered at either the departmental level, or in the forms of pay or course release for learning and teaching with technologies. But teaching with technologies does not necessarily mean teaching multimodality; for example, in the old survey, some people indicated that teaching with technology meant teaching in a computer classroom, which does not necessarily mean that multimodal composition is taught. Finally, both surveys revealed that some of the rewards come from intrinsic satisfaction of seeing students succeed, some recognition in teaching awards, and a component to be included in annual review documents. One comment in my survey said that they were invited to provide further training at presemester orientation meetings, which they did not see as a reward. Certainly, these recognitions are important, but if participating in trainings to teaching multimodality also leads to giving such training but not pay or course release, then it simply requires more labor and effort from the instructor, which may be difficult or problematic.

Discussion of Findings

In this study, I set out to investigate the "state of the field" on multimodal composition in writing programs and professional development support writing instructors rely on for teaching multimodality, and how their labor is valued in that process. Even though this is a limited, convenience sample, the research results provide a snapshot of the current state of how the teaching of multimodal composition is supported in a variety of writing programs and institutions. These findings present interesting implications for writing program administration work: how do we provide professional support for writing instructors on teaching multimodality, and how should we take advantage of already existing professional and social networks? They may also lead us to become more conscious about labor issues in our writing programs. Who should be performing the labor of professional development? How should we value the participation in these PD efforts? Before discussing the implications of this study for WPA work, I will first summarize the main findings:

- Multimodal composition plays an increasingly important role in our writing curricula across the nation. But the extent to which multimodality is implemented in writing classes is still very dependent on types of courses, programmatic and institutional contexts, as well as the preferences of individual instructors. Sometimes, within the same department or program, instructors may hold different opinions on the values of teaching multimodality.
- There still exists a spectrum of different perceptions on how multimodal writing should be defined, especially in relation to traditional print-based writing. While some instructors already assume the importance of multimodal composition and have moved beyond tool–oriented concerns to a more in-depth and critical understanding of the tools used, others still believe that multimodal writing is displacing important traditional writing practices.
- We now have more textbooks on teaching multimodal composition, but many instructors still compile their own teaching resources. There is also a need for texts that address more the cultural and social understanding of technologies (perhaps to support the students' development of critical literacies that Stuart Selber argued; see Pignetti and Inman) as well as new, emerging genres. Instructors often take on much individual responsibility and freedom on selecting their own teaching materials.
- Across institutions, we tend to provide inadequate and/or irregular and inconsistent formal professional development and training opportunities at both the programmatic level and the institutional level. Instructors are thus still largely more reliant on self-support to implement multimodal composition in their classes.
- Teaching multimodal composition and participating in professional development activities is sometimes recognized but hardly ever rewarded with pay or course releases.

These conclusions also align with the findings of *Inside Higher Education's* 2017 survey on faculty's attitudes on technology where online learning and use of digital technologies have been increasingly accepted by faculty, but not enough institutional professional support is provided for them. They still primarily rely on peer support with the use of these tools (Lederman and McKenzie).

These issues present challenges for WPAs and writing program administration in general. With the increasing presence and the importance of teaching multimodal literacies, instructors are often faced with the constraints of lack of teaching materials and professional support. At the same time, tensions within programs/department may exist due to different beliefs on such importance. For writing program administrators, how to better advocate for the values of multimodal composition and how to provide or support effective professional development efforts that take advantage of individual instructor experiences and expertise become important questions. The findings of my survey indicate that instructors are very much self-reliant in developing their pedagogies in multimodal literacies; they seek out the increasing number of teaching resources and materials as well as their professional and social networks for ideas and learning new technologies. So how can we take advantage of models of "self-training" and "learning from friends and colleagues informally" to foster the teaching of multimodality at the programmatic and institutional level?

Conclusion: Toward Social Learning Models of PD

At the national level, PD efforts for teaching multimodality are exemplified by CWIC /DMAC initiatives, which have been taking advantage of social learning models to construct communities of practice that supported integrating technologies into the writing classrooms—"informed by composition and rhetorical theory, educational theory, and technological understandings"—for over thirty years (DeVoss, Ball, Selfe, and DeWitt). Many people who have attended CIWIC/DMAC have taken away valuable peer learning experiences that supported teaching in their respective institutions (see special issue 36 of *Computers and Composition* and *Computers and Composition Online*).

I argue that we can apply such social learning models and approaches at the local level as well, as already done by some participants of DMAC institutes (DeJoy; McGrath and Guglielmo; Alexander and Williams). Here, based on my survey findings, I theorize a framework with some specific suggestions for us to consider how these issues overlap in our professional development efforts:

- PD efforts must be framed as intellectual endeavors with a combination of theory and practice. They must start with the theoretical foundations: departmental/programmatic conversations about multimodal composition with formalized expectations such as programmatic learning outcomes: how it is defined, and how it should be implemented.
- PD efforts should tap into the resources and experiences of individual instructors, allowing everyone to contribute to a department/program–wide knowledge base such as resource repositories including teaching materials, scholarly resources, assessment tools, composing tools, etc.
- PD efforts must create sustained peer learning communities that facilitate dialogues among all instructors for "distributed invention" (Alexander and Williams) on pedagogical practices such as designing assignments, planning lessons, and dealing with classroom challenges when teaching multimodality.
- PD efforts must be consistently assessed to address institutional and programmatic as well as students' needs in order to further improve PD activities on teaching multimodality.
- PD efforts should be properly recognized and compensated. WPAs should advocate for merit-based as well as material compensation such as pay or course release for those taking leadership positions in PD efforts, and also recognize the labor of participating and attending PD activities to improve their pedagogies. Programmatic policy languages should be created to clearly indicate methods of recognition and compensation, keeping in mind especially the precarious positions of contingent faculty.

At the programmatic level, we should inform and engage instructors in understanding both the theoretical and practical values of multimodal literacies, both broadly and in local contexts fitting particular programmatic and curricular goals. Just as many writing programs tend to adopt a selection of textbooks or even mandate instructional materials, crowdsourcing instructional materials on teaching multimodality may help provide better support for instructors. Increasingly, instructors are looking for materials that not only address the production of multimodal projects, but also address the critical and cultural dimensions of new media (as shown in the survey results). Searching in and across institutions and programs, crowdsourcing may be formalized and systematized at the programmatic level to be offered to instructors so that they do not have to rely so much on self-training and so that individual learning can have a social impact.

Willard-Traub argues that faculty development should be "an opportunity for reciprocal exchange, learning, and knowledge production" (434). Social and peer learning models can better enact such goals. Framing PD efforts as intellectual endeavors, WPAs may facilitate small peer learning groups among instructors that engage in activities of exchanging ideas and practices in teaching at different points of the semester. McGrath and Guglielmo emphasize the values of a community of practice model to professional development workshops in their own institution through "collaborative problem solving, peer learning, and information and strategy sharing during the workshop sessions and in the workshop space on the learning management system" (48). Alexander and Williams theorize the concept of "distributed invention" based on their experiences at DMAC to include "social, mutually appropriated, epistemic, negotiated, situated, proximal, responsive, interruptive, transformative, trust-based, and idiosyncratic" (38), which can be valuable to institutional professional development for writing instructors as well.

In this social process to support teaching, not only should instructors be in dialogue with one another, they must also relate their work to the needs of students. For example, University of Texas at El Paso's curriculum redesign approach to FYC involves all instructors in the decision-making process throughout the semester and takes advantage of different levels of experiences and expertise to redesign the program, in this productive community (Brunk-Chavez). In a similar vein, the New Media Writing Studio at Texas Christian University also presents an administrative model that values collaborative learning, especially in supporting the teaching of multimodal composing where a community of tenure-track faculty, full-time faculty, and graduate students in English collaborate to provide consultation and support for faculty teaching new media writing across disciplines.

These examples illustrate that successful social learning communities among instructors require intentional, meaningful, and sustainable professional development efforts. The inconsistencies in my survey findings reflect that consistent, formalized PD efforts must also address a variety of issues related to multimodal composing and pedagogies, bringing together theory and practice. To ensure a democratic process and increase sustainability of such structures, these groups should be formed and framed with clearly laid out goals and purposes and may be assessed with informal check-in points to ensure their effectiveness. Certainly, assessment of multimodal composition and related PD efforts is a complicated and at times challenging process. The model of digital writing assessment that involves students to cultivate experimentation and risk (see Reilly and Atkins) can also be applied to assessment of PD initiatives. What counts as effective

PD support for teaching multimodality? The answer to this question may look different from institution to institution and instructor to instructor. It is all the more important that the logistics of carrying out such efforts should be planned and discussed with a program committee with input from instructors themselves, especially when many of the instructors may be contingent faculty.

Thus, as we explore the possibilities of social learning models I recommend here, we need to critically examine the power dynamics in our institutional contexts and strive to enact these models in PD work in truly dialogic ways as intended. As Lind and Mullin argue, "all academic workers [need to] reconsider the stakes that necessitate supportive collaboration, recognition, and rewards" (14). When we ask faculty to participate in professional development activities, we are also asking them to put in more labor in their work (see Rodrigo and Romberger's work on the invisible service of "writing program technologists"). Many contingent faculty may also be very well prepared to lead PD efforts, but simply don't due to various factors such as department cultures, institutional policies, or consequently poor working conditions that rob them of the energy or agency to do so. How can we acknowledge and reward those who lead and attend these PD workshops? How do we build a peer learning community that's led by the peer instructors themselves? This may require the kind of resolution that Khan, Lalicker, and Lynch-Biniek call for to fight the exploitation of contingent faculty as well as a reframing of that rhetoric of exploitation into "a rhetoric of expectations and standards" that Babb and Wooten argue for, which emphasizes the importance of creating opportunities for contingent faculty "through collaborative involvement in programmatic decisions" (Babb and Wooten 170). Social learning models should be community based and continually evaluated based on the lived experiences of writing teachers in the local contexts.

Finally, I argue that we need to continue to assess, on the local and national level, how we teach multimodality in the writing curricula and how that teaching is supported by our institutional and professional structures by continuing to conduct empirical research, or what Haswell calls RAD research: replicable, aggregable, and data-based research. As of the publication of this article, more than fifteen years have passed since the old survey was launched. Browsing through prominent journals in the field on multimodal and digital composition like *Kairos* and *Computers and Composition*, we can see trajectories of development of multimodal composing, especially since 2005 when writing teachers have increasingly been exploring different ways of composing, be it hypertext or new media (see *Kairos* 10.2 on New Writing and Computer Technologies and *Computers and Composition* 25.1 on media convergence); writing online (see *Computers and Composition* 27.1); or other modes such as sound writing (see *Computers and Composition* 23.3) or writing and reading with games (*Computers and Composition* 25.3 and *Computers and Composition Online* fall 2008 issue), and issues such as freeware and accessibility (*Computers and Composition Online* fall 2009 special issue). Starting in 2003, *Kairos* has begun publishing a Praxis section, which over the years has offered many practical examples of how to teach multimodality in the writing classroom. At the same time, instructors and WPAs alike tried to push multiliteracies in the writing classroom, working with limitations of technology/internet access, advocating for changes and resources (see Takayoshi and Huot). As the access to technological resources improves in our classes and with the increasing trend of moving writing classes online (if only accelerated by the COVID-19 pandemic), we continue to be presented with challenges of fully integrating multimodality in all our classrooms and of ensuring productive professional development as well. In addition, multimodal composition is also tightly connected with issues of circulation and public writing as we take up new genres and networked technologies in our classrooms. We may also take advantage of networked tools for professional development such as Twitter or Slack, which can offer new ways of collaborative learning and socializing of teachers other than traditional workshops. As we look into the future of multimodality, I think we will need to critically consider the materiality of our composing processes, tools, contexts, both in our classrooms and in how we engage with programmatic professional development efforts.

Works Cited

Alexander, Kara Poe, and Danielle M. Williams. "DMAC After Dark: Toward a Theory of Distributed Invention." *Computers and Composition*, vol. 36, 2015, pp. 32–43, doi:10.1016/j.compcom.2015.04.001.

Anderson, Daniel, Anthony Atkins, Cheryl Ball, Krista Homicz, Cynthia Selfe, and Richard Selfe. "Integrating Multimodality into Composition Curricula: Survey Methodology and Results from a CCCC Research Grant." *Composition Studies*, vol. 34, no. 2, 2006, pp. 59–84.

Arola, Kristin L., Cheryl E. Ball, and Jennifer Sheppard. "Multimodal as a Frame for Individual and Institutional Change." *Hybrid Pedagogy*, 10 Jan. 2014. http://hybridpedagogy.org/multimodality-frame-individual-institutional-change/. Accessed 21 Apr 2018.

Arola, Kristin L., Jennifer Shepard, and Cheryl E. Ball. *Writer/Designer: A Guide to Making Multimodal Projects*. Bedford/St. Martin's, 2014.

Babb, Jacob, and Courtney Adams Wooten. "Traveling on the Assessment Loop: The Role of Contingent Labor in Curriculum Development." *Contingency,*

Exploitation, and Solidarity: Labor and Action in English Composition, edited by Seth Kahn, William B. Lalicker, and Amy Lynch-Biniek, 2017, pp. 169–82.

Brunk-Chavez, Beth. "Embracing Our Expertise through Faculty and Instructional Development." *WPA: Writing Program Administration,* vol. 34, no. 1, 2010, pp. 148–65.

Clark, J. Elizabeth. "The Digital Imperative: Making the Case for a 21st-Century Pedagogy." *Computers and Composition,* vol. 27, no. 1, 2010, pp. 27–35, doi:10.1016/j.compcom.2009.12.004.

DeJoy, Nancy C. "Faculty Development, Service Learning, and Composition: A Communal Approach to Professional Development." *Reflections: A Journal of Writing, Service-Learning, and Community Literacy,* vol. 1, no. 2, 2000, pp. 30–34.

DeVoss, Dànielle Nicole, Cheryl E. Ball, Cynthia L. Selfe, and Scott Lloyd DeWitt. "Letter from the Guest Editors." *Computers and Composition,* vol. 36, 2015, pp. v–viii, doi:10.1053/j.semnuclmed.2019.03.002.

Haswell, Richard. H. "NCTE/CCCC's Recent War on Scholarship." *Written Communication,* vol. 22, no. 2, 2005, pp. 198–223.

Hawisher, Gail E., and Cynthia L. Selfe, editors. *Passions, Pedagogies, and 21st Century Technologies.* Utah State UP and National Council of Teachers of English, 1999.

Hunter, Rik, Alana Frost, Moe Folk, and Les Loncharich. "Like Coming in From the Cold: Sponsors, Identities, and Technological Professional Development?" *Computers and Composition Online,* spring, 2015, http://cconlinejournal.org/ciwic_dmac/hunter-et-al.html. Accessed 10 Aug 2019.

Kahn, Seth, William B. Lalicker, and Amy Lynch-Biniek, editors. *Contingency, Exploitation, and Solidarity: Labor and Action in English Composition.* WAC Clearinghouse, 2017.

Kress, Gunther. *Literacy in the New Media Age.* Routledge, 2003.

Kress, Gunther, and Theo van Leeuwen. *Multimodal Discourse: The Modes and Media of Contemporary Communication.* Oxford UP, 2001.

Lalicker, William B., and Amy Lynch-Biniek. "Contingency, Solidarity, and Community Building: Principles for Converting Contingent to Tenure Track." *Contingency, Exploitation, and Solidarity: Labor and Action in English Composition,* edited by Seth Kahn, William B. Lalicker, and Amy Lynch-Biniek, 2017, pp. 91–102.

Lederman, Doug, and Lindsay McKenzie. "Faculty Buy-in Builds, Bit by Bit: Survey of Faculty Attitudes on Technology." *Inside Higher Ed,* 30 Oct 2017, https://www.insidehighered.com/news/survey/faculty-buy-builds-bit-bit-survey-faculty-attitudes-technology#.WgW4-q-MKTg.link. Accessed 10 Nov 2017.

Leverenz, Carrie S. "'Growing Smarter Over Time': An Emergence Model for Administrating a New Media Writing Studio." *Computers and Composition,* vol. 29, no. 1, 2012, pp. 51–62.

Lind, Carol, and Joan Mullin. "Silent Subversion, Quiet Competence, and Patient Persistence." *Contingency, Exploitation, and Solidarity: Labor and Action in Eng-*

lish Composition, edited by Seth Kahn, William B. Lalicker, and Amy Lynch-Biniek, 2017, pp. 13–26.

McGrath, Laura, and Letizia Guglielmo. "Communities of Practice and Makerspaces: DMAC's Influence on Technological Professional Development and Teaching Multimodal Composing." *Computers and Composition,* vol. 36, 2015, pp. 44–53.

Mina, Lilian W. *First-Year Composition Teachers' Uses of New Media Technologies in the Composition Class.* Dissertation, Indiana University of Pennsylvania, 2014.

Pignetti, Daisy, and James A. Inman. "Selber, Stuart A. *Multiliteracies for a Digital Age.* Carbondale: Southern Illinois UP, 2004. 240 pp." *Composition Forum,* vol. 14, no. 2, 2005, http://compositionforum.com/issue/14.2/rev-selber.php. Accessed 5 Sept 2019.

Reilly, Colleen A., and Anthony T. Atkins. "Rewarding Risk: Designing Aspirational Assessment Processes for Digital Writing Projects." *Digital Writing: Assessment and Evaluation,* edited by Heidi A. McKee and Dànielle Nicole DeVoss, Computers and Composition Digital Press/Utah State University Press, 2013, https://ccdigitalpress.org/book/dwae/04_reilly.html. Accessed 21 Dec 2020.

Rodrigo, Rochelle, and Julia Romberger. "Managing Digital Technologies in Writing Programs: Writing Program Technologists & Invisible Service." *Computers and Composition,* vol. 44, 2017, pp. 67–82.

Selfe, Cynthia L., editor. *Multimodal Composition: Resources for Teachers,* Hampton Press, 2007.

Selfe, Cynthia L., and Gail E. Hawisher. *Literate Lives in the Information Age: Narratives of Literacy from the United States.* Lawrence Erlbaum Associates, 2004.

Shipka, Jody. *Toward a Composition Made Whole.* U of Pittsburgh P, 2001.

Takayoshi, Pamela, and Brian Huot. "Composing in a Digital World: The Transition of a Writing Program and Its Faculty." *WPA: Writing Program Administration,* vol. 32, no. 3, 2009, pp. 89–120.

Takayoshi, Pamela, and Cynthia Selfe. "Multimodal Teaching." *Multimodal Composition: Resources for Teachers.* Hampton, 2007.

Willard-Traub, Margaret K. "Writing Program Administration and Faculty Professional Development: Which Faculty? What Development?" *Pedagogy: Critical Approaches to Teaching Literature, Language, Composition, and Culture,* vol. 8, no. 3, 2008, pp. 433–45.

WPA Outcomes Statement for First-Year Composition (3.0), Approved July 17, 2014. CWPA, 2014, http://wpacouncil.org/aws/CWPA/pt/sd/news_article/243055/_PARENT/layout_details/false. Accessed 21 Dec 2020.

Wysocki, Anne, Johndan Johnson-Eilola, Cynthia L. Selfe, and Geoffrey Sirc. *Writing New Media: Theory and Applications for Expanding the Teaching of Composition.* Utah State UP, 2004.

Yancey, Kathleen Blake. "Writing in the 21st Century: A Report from the National Council of Teachers of English." National Council of Teachers of English, 2009, http://www.ncte.org/library/NCTEFiles/Press/Yancey_final.pdf. Accessed 21 Dec 2020.

Chen Chen is Assistant Professor of English at Winthrop University in Rock Hill, South Carolina, where she teaches first-year writing and professional and technical communication courses. She received her Ph.D. in Communication, Rhetoric, and Digital Media from North Carolina State University. She studies how graduate students professionalize into the field of rhetoric and composition across different disciplinary spaces. Currently, she's also working on projects about Chinese feminist rhetorics and COVID-19 communications in transcultural contexts. Her other research interests are TPC pedagogies and course design, digital rhetoric, and social media.

The Tacit Values of Sourced Writing: A Study of Source "Engagement" and the FYW Program as Community of Practice

Donna Scheidt and Holly Middleton

Abstract

A writing program with high faculty autonomy adopted a new learning outcome emphasizing integration of sources and a related synthesis assignment with broad guidelines. In dynamic criteria mapping preceding assessment, program faculty in small group interviews valued "engagement" in student's sourced writing but could not reach consensus on what they meant. This study makes explicit these otherwise tacit values associated with students' sourced writing in FYW. In an attempt to operationalize "engagement," we compared the results of two processes: a program assessment conducted in 2012-13 of a simple random sample of students' sourced essays and collaborative coding of the same sample. Statistically significant correlations were found between high assessment scores and specific discursive moves such as summary, as well as frequency and variation in type of source use. These findings bring the professional judgement of writing teachers into relief and suggest that, despite its high autonomy and lack of a common assignment, this FYW program is functioning as an intermediary community of practice between individual classrooms and disciplinary contexts. There are significant implications for strengthening programmatic research and authority.

In many writing programs across the country, faculty share learning outcomes while enjoying a large degree of autonomy with respect to pedagogy and course design. Faculty autonomy is understandably cherished, but it can be perceived as posing challenges for programs' sense of coherence and consistency in focus. This perception is especially problematic to the extent that faculty would seem to lack a common understanding and enactment of student learning outcomes and the values that inform them, posing potential risks for fairness and consistency in assessment of student work. After all, articulating a student learning outcome rarely creates faculty consensus on its own terms, no matter the process of its formulation or the clarity of its statement. Thus, at the same time that faculty enjoy high levels of autonomy within a writing program, their authority may be undermined unless the coherence of what they know and value as a community—their professional expertise with respect to learning outcomes—can be brought into relief.

Demonstrating a writing program's coherence with respect to outcomes is also critical to program assessment, curricular revision, and programmatic authority. This is especially true when a program is weak along the lines of what Finer and White-Farnham (2017) called architecture, "the institutional structures that, alongside its people, anchor a program to the ground and keep it standing" (p. 4). Such architecturally weak programs often rely on the person of the WPA to accomplish assessment and program revision, enabling institutional flexibility. Authority concerning hiring, scheduling, budgeting, and evaluating full-time teaching faculty is frequently lodged with a third-party, such as a department chair. Consistent with Gladstein and Regaignon's (2012) research on small liberal arts colleges, however, a WPA may have considerable influence on these and other decisions (if not the authority to sign off on them) as well as with the chair and faculty in other disciplines. An important part of this influence is leadership on assessment. Program assessment has the potential to especially heighten a WPA's influence within an architecturally weak writing program so long as that WPA can demonstrate programmatic coherence and consistency and lift up the collective professional expertise of writing faculty, which is potentially challenging when a writing program also invites high levels of faculty autonomy.

Such were the salient circumstances and challenges in fall 2012, as we worked within a writing program at High Point University, a small private comprehensive university with a liberal arts mission. Holly serves as WPA; she is a tenured faculty member who at the time received a course release during the academic year and a stipend to conduct assessment and program revision over the summer. Donna is also a teured faculty member who periodically teaches within the program, but was not doing so at the time of this study. As a potential further challenge to program coherence and consistency, instructors collectively adopted a new learning outcome earlier in the spring, emphasizing students' integration of others' ideas and information. By fall, a new required synthesis assignment was introduced with very general guidelines regarding word and source counts. There was not yet a shared understanding of the synthesis assignment's purpose or methods for teaching and grading it given high instructor autonomy, combined with the new integration outcome. Under these circumstances—high faculty autonomy, a relatively new learning outcome, very general shared assignment requirements—we wondered: could this writing program be understood as operating with a sense of shared values, particularly with respect to a new outcome?

This overarching question motivated us to explore faculty's understanding of how students effectively integrated others' ideas and information in their writing. Furthermore, we wanted to know the extent to which faculty judgments could be described as coherent and consistent with respect to this outcome. We investigated what program faculty valued in students' integration of sources through a small-group professional development activity known as dynamic criteria mapping (DCM) and program assessment (both conducted by Holly). During DCM, a process that identifies the values in play in the teaching and assessment of student writing (Broad, 2009), faculty frequently invoked "engagement" during discussion, but the term was so fluid it could not be defined for use in assessment of source integration. Assessment nevertheless proceeded with the criteria and vocabulary that could be derived from DCM, with a committee of eight writing instructors scoring 51 essays, a random sample of source essays taken from fall 2012 first-year writing (FYW) courses. This led us to the research question we explore here: what do faculty mean by "engagement" with respect to student writing that integrates sources?

To answer this question, and to investigate whether faculty assessments of students' integration of sources could be captured consistently through different means, we employed a second process. In this second process, using over half of the same random sample of student essays, we collaboratively coded students' discursive moves and compared our results with the scores assigned to those essays during assessment. We found statistically significant correlations between high assessment scores and specific moves such as summary as well as variation and frequency in type of source use. These findings made explicit, for us, what Geisler (1994) has termed the "tacit rhetorical dimension" and what Lancaster (2016) has termed the "discursive consciousness" of academic writing. By describing discursive moves specific to high-scoring essays, we also affirm that our FYW program is functioning as a community of practice, which specifically emphasizes "practices and values that hold communities together" while acknowledging the importance of texts, genres, and language of significance to discourse communities (Johns, 1997, p. 52).

While FYW programs are often described as communities, the more precise phrase "community of practice" is often reserved for courses in the disciplines and majors. If a FYW program were functioning as a community of practice, we would expect to see its values evident in the ways that student writing is read by faculty, particularly during recurring communal practices like program assessment. Our findings suggest that our FYW program is functioning as a community of practice, and our methods offer a map for how other programs might uncover their own tacit values and strengthen their programs. For us, this study foregrounded tacit knowledge that we can teach as explicit practice: a sense of what Lancaster (2016) called the "formation of an academic stance" and Brent (2013) called "a shift . . . to what the writer *does*" in relation to individual sources. In the language of thresholds, we uncovered "the assumptions of a community of practice" (Adler-Kassner & Wardle, 2015) associated with sourced writing in FYW.[1] By emphasizing variation in source use, we are also in conversation with Harris's *Rewriting* (2017) and Bizup's (2008) work on rhetorical use ("BEAM"). We took a term that described the most valuable aspect of faculty's reading experience of sourced essays—"engagement"—and worked to identify its textual features.

Through these two processes—assessing and coding the same sample of student writing—our work offers a way to integrate WPA work on teaching, learning, and assessment as a research agenda. While writing assessment has only grown as a field of inquiry over the past two decades, it is often subject to the same local pressure described by Anson and Brown (1999): "much programmatic research is conducted by professional staff members . . . whose own credibility and job status are determined largely by how well they support the operation of the institution," rather than student learning or the scholarship required for tenure and promotion (p. 144).

This kind of research also can institutionally strengthen programs by bringing writing teachers' expertise into relief. As Gallagher (2011) argued in "Being There," "only we—faculty and students—are in a position to improve teaching and learning in meaningful ways" (p. 468), and conducting meaningful assessment develops and makes visible the expertise of those who teach in the program. In programs with weak architectures like ours, controlling assessment can therefore strengthen not only teaching and learning but also the structure of the program itself. That our program functions as a community of practice is also important for this reason. It anticipates and responds to the criticism that writing grades are subjective by demonstrating the consistency and coherence of professional judgement.

Below we first articulate our framework, then outline our methods, design, and findings. We conclude with research, pedagogical, and programmatic implications.

A COMMUNITY OF PRACTICE FRAMEWORK:
VALUES, DISCOURSES, AND PRACTICES

Because the community of practice model is not an operating framework, we found inconsistent attention in the literature to communal contexts, in particular to how faculty read and value the discourses of FY students' sourced writing as part of routine program practice. What academic writers at different levels value (or understand or think) about working with sources differs, and these values in turn shape the practices (or strategies) with which they compose. More experienced writers tend to value sourced writing as inquiry or "knowledge-transforming" (Scardamalia & Bereiter, 1987) and as "open-ended and interpretive" (Schwegler & Shamoon, 1982, p. 820). In contrast, less experienced writers typically understand sourced writing as "a close-ended, informative, skills-oriented exercise" (p. 820), adopting practices consistent with a model of composing that has been termed "knowledge-telling" according to which writers largely replicate or report on what they know or learn (Scardamalia & Bereiter, 1987).

Our understanding of students' work with sources is informed by rich discourse analyses of stance, or how a writer orients to their materials or sources. Professional writers often employ "evidentials of citation" by using verbs such as *"say, report, show,* and *demonstrate"* to signal the work of sources (Barton, 1993, p. 751), thereby exercising "a means of appropriating the literature rather than simply citing it" (p. 752). In their analysis of 4,032 first-year directed self-placement essays and 615 upper-division and graduate student A-graded essays at two institutions, Aull and Lancaster (2014) found clear developmental trajectories in the metadiscursive construction of stance. The cohorts at both institutions shared distinctive patterns, with first-year writers especially struggling to construct a "sufficiently honed and cautious stance in a community of many views (cited or not)" (p. 173). A later study by Lancaster (2016) reiterated the importance of cautious stance-taking in academic writing, discovering that a corpus of philosophy essays included frequent discursive devices associated with "confident uncertainty," especially "hedging" (p. 131). Knowledge of these discursive attributes proved tacit, however, to both an undergraduate major and a professor in philosophy who described their writing not as cautious but direct and assertive.

The studies discussed above have much to offer as points of departure for our own work. In general, though, their evaluation of the discursive attributes of student writing underappreciates how the values they reflect are typically embedded in practice—for our purposes, acts of reading undertaken by faculty operating within programmatic contexts, reading and valuing student texts with certain learning outcomes and other programmatic purposes (like assessment) in mind. For example, studies commonly draw on non-naturalistic prompts, often in timed settings geared toward placement or proficiency testing (e.g., Aull & Lancaster, 2014; Barton, 1993), or favor one or two aspects of a community over others. (For example, Flower [1990b] prioritized studying students' metacognitive awareness and practices over their discourses). With certain recent exceptions (e.g., Lancaster, 2016), linguistically oriented studies largely have emphasized students' written discourses and seem to assume that other aspects (values, practices) can be understood directly by the researchers' analyses of these discourses.

These studies nevertheless contributed productively to longstanding debates about the genre of the "research paper" in FYW (Davis & Shadle, 2000; Larson, 1982; Melzer & Zemlianksy, 2003), challenging the idea that a particular genre of writing regularly falls short of meaningful or academically valued work with sources (see, e.g., Flower, 1990a on "critical literacy"). With regard to the genres of FYW in particular, some have taken this point so far as to argue that genres like the research paper are without value altogether unless embedded in disciplinary contexts (Beaufort, 2007; Wardle, 2009). Yet this perspective warrants reconsideration given a growing body of research describing with nuance how students work discursively with sources as well as the meaningful research and writing experiences that students can have in FYW (Eodice, Geller, & Lerner, 2016).

We therefore sought to discover how the discourses, practices, and values associated with sourced writing relate by highlighting the contexts and communities in which sourced writing takes place. Describing the research paper as a "fundamentally important genre," Brent (2013) asserted that this genre of sourced writing is defined by "what a community—in this case, the community of people who teach writing and of students who learn to write—perceive as a commonly recurring exigence that is responded to in certain commonly recurring ways" (p. 36). Brent helpfully shifted here from a genre of sourced writing to those academic communities in which this genre might serve as a meaningful discursive practice. Informed by this shift, we believe that an intermediary community—the FYW program—deserves greater attention, existing as it does between individual classrooms and disciplinary contexts.

Method

Campus Context

A private comprehensive university located in the southeastern United States, High Point University offers a broad range of undergraduate degrees, including those in the traditional liberal arts, business, furniture and interior design, exercise science, and education; graduate degrees are offered in business, communication, education, and the health professions. For the academic year 2012–13, the university enrolled 3,926 undergraduate students, 1,257 of which were FY students. While the percentage has increased every year since, in 2012 only 13% of total enrolled students belonged to a self-identified minority group (HPU Office of Research and Planning, 2018, p. 19). For the 2018–19 academic year, passing rates and average grades between "all ENG 1103 students" and ENG 1103 students belonging to a self-identified minority group indicate no significant differences; in any given semester, almost all students pass the FYW requirement.

Most students satisfy the university-mandated writing requirement by enrolling in ENG 1103: College Writing and Public Life, a one-semester FYW course housed in an English department with specializations in rhetoric and composition, literature, and creative writing. At the beginning of the fall 2012 semester, 562 students were enrolled across twenty-five sections of FYW. Of these students, 408 consented to participate in this study, which is part of a larger collaborative research project investigating undergraduate research and writing approved by the university's Institutional Review Board (Upward Project, 2018).[2]

Formative Outcomes Assessment Process

In April 2012, FYW instructors condensed a long list of CWPA learning outcomes to be more responsive to institutional general education requirements. One result was a stronger emphasis on integration of sources as a shared outcome: "Conduct research as inquiry, in the sense of . . . integrating others' ideas and information with one's own." The writing program subsequently conducted formative assessment of integration but did not yet share an assignment that required students to integrate sources in writing. The following guidelines were therefore introduced in fall 2012 for a new required synthesis assignment: (1) it must be an essay of 1200–1400 words and (2) it must integrate at least three sources.

Instructors in the writing program experience a large degree of autonomy with respect to pedagogy and course design. The writing program is staffed by an array of English department faculty: long-time adjunct instructors (on semester contracts), full-time instructors (on one-year contracts), and tenured/tenure-track faculty who rotate into teaching FYW. All faculty have advanced degrees in English and have knowledge of and experience with best practices in teaching rhetorical approaches to writing. High instructor autonomy, combined with the new integration outcome, meant there was not yet a shared understanding of the synthesis assignment's purpose or methods for teaching and grading it. To generate such an understanding, instructors designed and shared their assignments for sourced writing.

Formative outcomes assessment was therefore undertaken in order to generate a shared working vocabulary for program values and to inform curricular revision. In fall 2012, the WPA (Holly) identified a simple random sample of 60 students enrolled in ENG 1103 who had agreed to participate in the study. A work study student collected 51 of their synthesis essays and replaced identifying information with a code. The essays were divided among four packets, each of which was assigned two faculty readers on the outcomes assessment committee.

Early in 2013, Holly conducted dynamic criteria mapping (DCM), a process that identifies the values in play in the teaching and assessment of student writing (Broad, 2009). Holly first led small-group interviews with all English department faculty. In groups of five, participants were presented with the same two student essays and asked to identify what they did and did not value in each student's work with sources. Based on minutes compiled from these meetings, Holly developed a criteria map. Over several meetings in April and May, the eight members of the assessment committee revised this map into the glossary eventually used as the assessment rubric. (For the rubric, please see Upward Project [2018].)

Along with Holly, three tenured/tenure-track faculty, two full-time instructors, and two adjunct instructors across all specializations comprised the assessment committee. (Donna was not involved with assessment.) For the assessment procedure, paired members of the assessment committee scored the same packet using the finalized worksheet and glossary. Readers were asked to assign each essay an integration score using a 1–6 scale, where 1–3 signified degrees of failure to meet expectations for the outcome and 4–6 signified degrees of meeting expectations. The 1–6 scale was selected to yield more meaningful data and to compel debate about what constitutes the distinction between a 3 (not proficient) and 4 (proficient) performance. The paired readers' 1–6 integration scores were combined into what we call a total integration score of 2–12. No scores were thrown out and no third readers were brought in to adjudicate. For each 1–6 score, readers selected the value-neutral criterion from the glossary that most informed their judgement. The glossary thus served as the central assessment instrument.

During the faculty small group interviews about student writing, engagement emerged as an important value. But because it could not be specifically defined—it could variously mean engagement with sources, with the subject, with the reader, or simply involvement—the term was not added to the glossary. This assessment context gave rise to our interest in engagement as something writing faculty read for, a valued quality of the reading experience but one with slippery textual referents. As we discussed what was for us an interesting problem our research questions took shape:

what do we mean by engagement with sources in student writing? What moves do FYW students make when they engage with a source?

Study Design

We pursued these questions at the August 2013 Dartmouth Summer Seminar for Composition Research where we attempted to operationalize "engagement" by developing a coding scheme for the essays collected for assessment in fall 2012. However, in order to ensure that each essay was in fact responding to a writing prompt calling for a synthesis essay, we devised the following two rules: (1) the assignment had to require three or more sources and (2) the primary learning goal of the assignment had to be synthesis.

Of the original 51 essays procured from the sample, 35 essay assignments (69%) conformed to the rules; of these, 33 were coded. Rhetorical moves occur at the level of the t-unit (Geisler, 2018, p. 224), so each essay was then segmented by t-unit onto an Excel spreadsheet by row.

To generate preliminary codes, we collaboratively coded three essays chosen at random from the sample. After reading through the data individually performing what Saldaña (2009) described as "initial coding" (p. 81)—making notes about patterns and themes that might offer "analytic leads for further exploration" (p. 81)—we discussed results. Work with the initial three essays helped us identify when students engaged with sources as "source referentiality." We therefore coded as a "reference" any t-unit in which the writer made explicit reference to a source, usually through citation practice, attribution, or acknowledgment of authorship (see Jamieson, 2017, on difficulties of determining how to code for sources in student texts). We came to define a "source" as any alphabetic text, in digital or print format, that is either included in the bibliography of a student essay, or that a reader would expect to see so included.

In order to capture both the reference to a source and the type of engagement with that source, we created what Geisler (2004) calls a "nested" coding scheme (p. 90) that required two rounds. In the first round, we coded the writer's reference to a source (source referentiality, what we referred to as dimension 1) and in the second round coded each of these instances a second time for source engagement, whether or not the attempt was considered successful (dimension 2). Codes for source engagement captured what students did with sources—their discursive moves—rather than their metadiscourse through which they might signal their academic stance or orientation to their sources (e.g., through hedging or using certain verbs). We generated five categories of source engagement based on work with the initial three essays: Inform, Explain, React, Develop, and Connect. We then further refined the definitions and boundaries of these categories by applying the codes to two new essays. A preliminary test of reliability with a third coder not involved with the study produced very high agreement (98% simple agreement) on source referentiality, giving us confidence that our description of source referentiality (dimension 1) was well defined. This coder, however, produced more moderate agreement (68% simple agreement) on source engagement. Granted, a "correct" coding requires two levels of accuracy with respect to source referentiality (dimension 1) as well as source engagement (dimension 2). Conversely, any errors in coding for referentiality will necessarily carry over as errors for engagement, reducing the rate of agreement for this second dimension. Even so, this coder's robust rate of agreement for referentiality meant that agreement in codes with respect to source engagement was little affected; the relatively low level of agreement for engagement signaled a need to further refine the codes for dimension 2.

In the revised coding scheme, the types of dimension 2 source engagement were defined as follows:

- **Inform:** the writer refers to discrete or specific information, facts, definitions, etc.
- **Explain:** the writer summarizes, paraphrases, or integrates or refers to a quote that demonstrates awareness of a source or its author beyond mere facts: as having something significant to say, as doing at least minimal argumentative or rhetorical work, or as having a means or method of saying something.
- **React:** the writer reacts to or takes a position in relation to a source, regardless of accuracy. React is primarily reactive rather than generative.
- **Develop:** the writer builds upon or analyzes ideas from the source.
- **Connect:** the writer makes connections between two (or more) texts or two (or more) authors.

For the coding schemes, please see Upward Project (2018).

Another independent coder not directly involved with the study was asked to code the three essays. This coder produced more moderate agreement with respect to source referentiality (82% simple agreement) and similarly moderate agreement with respect to source engagement (76% simple agreement). When the automatic dimension 2 error (described above) was removed, however, agreement as to source engagement proved stronger (86% simple agreement) and within the 85–90% minimal benchmark range Saldaña (2009, p. 28) and Geisler (2004, p. 84) recommended for interrater reliability. Based on these reliability results, we moved forward with coding 33 of the remaining essays, with each researcher coding roughly half. Questions and issues were discussed as they arose in order to reach consensus and enhance "intercoder agreement" (Saldaña, 2009, pp. 27–28; Smagorinsky, 2008, p. 401).

Despite being composition-rhetoric faculty members in the same English department teaching the same course to the same student body, we revised our coding scheme several times over many months to arrive at one reliable enough to proceed. As such, our code development was the sort of process that Serviss (2017) suggested invites reflection. Because we could not agree on how to code—how to simply describe what the writer was doing—the scope of what we initially thought we might capture had to be continually narrowed. We understand the multiplicity of meanings cued by these student texts as attesting to not only the elusiveness of language but also the composing practices of individual readers and the resulting specificity that coding requires. Nevertheless, the final scheme demonstrates an engagement similar to the rhetorical functions Bizup outlined in his BEAM taxonomy (2008) and evokes Toulmin's argumentative framework, especially as adapted to investigations of students' textual source use (Beaufort, 2007; Haller, 2010).

Discussion of Results

We found several statistically significant correlations between essays assigned high scores via assessment and certain coding patterns. For example, faculty value specific ways in which students engage with sources. When students Explain a source, they summarize, paraphrase, or integrate that source, or they refer to a quote in a way that demonstrates an awareness of the source as authored. The more students Explain sources in their essays, the more faculty value their essays (p =.002, a highly statistically significant correlation).[3] This was also true of Develop—building upon or analyzing ideas from sources (p =.062, a statistically significant correlation at .10 level)[4]—and Connect—making connections between two or more texts or authors (p =.030, a statistically significant correlation).[5] No statistically significant relationship was shown, however, between the number of times a student Informs or Reacts to sources in an essay and how faculty scored the essay. In particular, Informing is frequently used by students as a group, but without a statistically significant relationship to faculty assessment scores (p =.682).[6] The more a student engages with sources in any of these three specific ways—Explain, Develop, or Connect—the more highly a student's essay was scored during assessment.

There is also a highly statistically significant relationship between the number of different ways a student engages in an essay and the faculty assessment score that essay receives ($p =.010$).[7] In other words, an essay that Informs and Explains and Reacts and Develops and Connects is more likely to be valued by faculty than an essay that engages sources in just two or three of these ways. We use the term "variation" for this finding, to denote a demonstration of engaging sources in multiple ways.

Finally, our analysis demonstrates a highly statistically significant correlation between the number of times students engaged with sources in ways other than Inform—i.e., Explain, React, Develop, and Connect—and faculty's valuation of the essay ($p =.003$).[8] When we removed Inform and reanalyzed our data, we discovered a statistically significant correlation between frequency of source use and faculty assessment. We use the term "frequency" for this finding, to denote the rate at which sources are engaged, with the caveat that a high rate of source use is only valued when sources are used in ways more sophisticated than Inform. In other words, it is important to note that type of source use and frequency are connected here. There is a weak positive linear correlation between the total number of sources referenced in an essay and the essay's assessment score, but this relationship is not statistically significant ($p =.131$).[9] As described above, Inform created noise for purposes of frequency analysis because students often Inform, but Inform alone does not significantly correlate with assessment scores.

These findings clarify the features of sourced writing that FYW faculty value and the discursive contours of what is meant by the otherwise ill-defined term "engagement." Consistent with the existing literature, we found that faculty value certain discursive moves over others: e.g., when a student summarizes, paraphrases, or otherwise integrates a source in a way that demonstrates an awareness of an author or source (Explain). This finding is consistent with research demonstrating more experienced writers at the very least "appropriate the literature rather than simply citing it" (Barton, 1993, p. 8). To Explain a source at minimum preserves some sense of the rhetorical dimensions of a source as authored (Geisler, 1994). It is an alternative, however basic, to looking through the source and deploying it as information.

Faculty also value when a FYW student builds upon or analyzes ideas from sources (Develops) or makes connections between two or more texts or authors (Connects). This finding accords with corpus analysis research that found experienced writers more frequently elaborate or exemplify (with code glosses) and distinguish between opposing perspectives (with connectors) (Aull & Lancaster, 2014). The writer thus situates themselves with respect to other authors, informed by the rhetorical knowledge that agreement (and disagreement) is fluid among them (Geisler, 1994). As discursive moves, Develop and Connect also would appear to demonstrate what Flower (1990b) and Aull and Lancaster (2014) described as "complexity."

Similar to others, we found that faculty value the overall variety ("rhetorical source use" [Haller, 2010]) and frequency (e.g., Barton, 1993) with which students employ certain kinds of discursive moves. Students who work with sources in diverse ways and multiple times in an essay (in any way other than Inform) are considered to be engaging with sources. We suspect that Inform and React are valued when a part of variation (but not individually) because they are read as discursive moves that need to be made sense of or earned in relation to other types of engagement. That is, it is not enough for a student to Inform or React without a sense of why information is being provided or the basis for the writer's reaction, purposes advanced by Explaining, Connecting, and/or Developing. Altogether, these findings are suggestive of the discursive attributes of FY students' sourced writing associated with knowledge-transforming (Scardamalia & Bereiter, 1987) and inquiry (American Library Association, 2015; Schwegler & Shamoon, 1982) in FYW.

Our results provide some empirical support defining the contours of a notoriously nebulous term of art in the field of composition. This description and operationalization of source engagement is, of course, somewhat limited to the context of this study, shaped by the understanding and values of writing faculty involved in a particular program and teaching a minimally defined "synthesis" essay. However, our contribution is in developing a concrete scheme for FYW students' source engagement and demonstrating how we did so.

By clarifying faculty's tacit values about students' engagement with sources, we enrich conversations about the teaching of sourced writing. This study confirms findings from an earlier one in which we found that an important step toward inquiry was a FY writer's conscious choice to read and understand their sources (Scheidt et al., 2017). Our findings also contribute to other studies (e.g., Jamieson, 2017) heightening FYW faculty's awareness regarding the importance of academic literacies they might otherwise dismiss as "basic," like students' summary or even acknowledgment of a source or author (Jamieson, 2013). Faculty may therefore find tools like the vocabulary and findings of this study helpful to understanding both their students and themselves. Such tools can delineate the "tacit rhetorical dimension" (Geisler, 1994) or their own "discursive consciousness" (Lancaster, 2016) regarding reasonable academic expectations for FY sourced writing. While other, similar options exist (e.g., BEAM [Bizup, 2008]), the pedagogical implications of this study derive from research conducted with faculty reading and evaluating students' sourced writing as part of a community of practice.

As Adler-Kassner and Wardle (2015) reminded us, "Learning threshold concepts amounts to learning some of the assumptions of a community of practice" (p. 8), including those concepts meaningful for FYW (see Downs & Robertson, 2015). The FYW program here did not adopt the kind of curriculum typically associated with writing as a discipline or teaching for transfer; it was in a state of flux later given direction by instructors, assessment results, and research on writing assignments in required general education courses. Even so, it functioned with remarkable coherence among the values, practices, and discourses of source engagement, suggesting that FYW programs can be important sites for student writers in their development across the curriculum. As researchers studying attributes of writing sometimes assume that aspects of program context must be uniform—e.g., a standard syllabus, a shared assignment, etc.—our findings encourage expanding the possibilities for research in FYW.

Geisler (1994) noted the distinction between novices and experts is not simply cognitive but also social and cultural (p. 207). So understood, academic literacy includes a tacit rhetorical dimension that, while potentially informed by specific disciplinary and professional discourses, also can be explained in more general terms: this kind of academic literacy is slow, emerging fully only at advanced levels of professional training (p. 95), so that learning in the first year is likely to be modest. In this study, we give shape and definition to some of these modest aims toward cultivating academic literacy in the first year.

Conclusion

Our findings should encourage other researchers interested in studying writing phenomena within the complicated, everyday contexts of writing programs. At the same time, the study also raises an interesting conceptual question for this kind of research: how flexible is this notion of community of practice? How far does it stretch before findings are no longer meaningful, complicated to too great a degree by too many confounding factors? Despite the complexities of its naturalistic setting, our study provides a means of systematically pursuing this line of inquiry.

We bring attention to the role of faculty perspective in sourced writing instruction by identifying the features of source engagement that they value: Explaining, Developing, or Connecting, as well as when sources are engaged with more variety and frequency (other than to Inform). So doing, we develop a concrete scheme for identifying when students engage sources in writing and how. Yet we suspect that it may not be the codes themselves that are useful in other contexts so much as the story of how they came to be, a point of departure we hope others might not so much reproduce as refine and make their own (Serviss, 2017, p. 5).

In subsequent years, Holly continued to conduct DCM to define the values at play in other learning outcomes and to embed assessment into the routine work of all faculty teaching FYW. All faculty participate in selecting the outcome to assess, while some serve on the committee designing the assessment, and a group of 4–8 finalize the design and conduct assessment each summer. As of this writing, a committee is conducting assessment of the outcome "find and evaluate sources," which serves the purpose of the main writing project: to conduct an inquiry that demonstrates variation in both source type (genre) and rhetorical use, a purpose defined by this study.

In conjunction with program assessment, our research clarified the underlying values of the program and helped strengthen them. Assessment thus also served as meaningful faculty development, enhancing faculty's understanding of themselves and their practices. For example, faculty valued summarizing, paraphrasing, or quoting with an awareness of author and source (Explain) more highly than they thought; our findings reframe a distaste for summary as a perceived overreliance on Inform or lack of variation. Perhaps most important, faculty gained confidence in their understanding of and judgments with respect to source engagement and the program gained a more precise shared vocabulary. This study maps one way to ensure that faculty are central to meaningfully improving teaching and learning (Gallagher, 2011), and to make faculty expertise visible to stakeholders as coherent professional judgment.

We bear in mind Lunsford's (2017) insight that these methods and codes are only "stabilized for now" (p. xviii), adding that, paradoxically, by using these results to inform curricular change we may have destabilized them. We began to explicitly teach different rhetorical uses for sources (Bizup, 2008; Wolfe, Olson, & Wilder, 2014) and made variation in source use a core requirement of the final research project. To create the conditions for meaningful research and writing experiences, that final project is now a semester-long inquiry based on an initial analysis of the student's choosing, often incorporating primary sources and research methods. These revisions mean that the same study could now yield different codes. Engagement may be an enduring and bedrock value for readers, but its meanings are not to be taken for granted.

We see FYW as an important and generative site for academic literacy. FYW programs can function as communities of practice where first-year students embark on the developmental trajectory of engaging sources with more depth, variety, and frequency. On this point, Aull and Lancaster (2014) have found, first-year students at different institutions may be more similar to each other than to the advanced students at their own. Crafting a "sufficiently honed and cautious stance in a community of many views" is their greatest shared difficulty in writing (p. 173) and a way of being in the world they will not master in one semester. Designing experiences where our students practice shaping and situating their own perspectives in relation to a variety of others is foundational work in the first year.

Acknowledgments

We wish to acknowledge Lisa Schmitz, MS, MA of Saint Paul College for conducting this project's statistical analysis. Participation in the Dartmouth Summer Seminar in Research Methods was funded by High Point University through a University Research Advancement Grant (Donna) and a Summer Scholar Award (Holly).

Notes

1. We adopt the phrases "writing from sources" and "sourced writing" somewhat interchangeably as a means of distinguishing our focus from the kind of academic writing commonly referred to as "research writing." Here, we do not assume that a FY writer has conducted independent research in the sense of finding sources.

2. Approved by High Point University's IRB under protocol number 201207-115.

3. Results of a simple linear regression with a dependent variable of total integration score and an independent variable of total number of references that Explain. With $n = 33$, the line of best fit showed the variables to be highly correlated (with correlation coefficient of .519), highly statistically significant at significance level of .05. The significance level is the same for all analyses unless otherwise stated.

4. Results of same analysis, correlation .329, statistically significant at level of significance .10.

5. Correlation .379.

6. Negative correlation (–.074), not statistically significant ($p = .682$).

7. Results of same analysis but with an independent variable of number of different types of engagement. Correlation .442.

8. Results of same analysis but with an independent variable of total number of references used not including Inform. Correlation .502. For scatter plot, see Upward Project (2018).

9. Result of same analysis but with an independent variable of total number of references used. Variables weakly correlated (with correlation coefficient of .268). For scatter plot, see Upward Project (2018).

REFERENCES

Adler-Kassner, Linda, & Wardle, Elizabeth A. (2015). *Naming what we know: Threshold concepts of writing studies.* Logan, UT: Utah State University Press.

American Library Association. (2015, February 9). Framework for information literacy for higher education. http://www.ala.org/acrl/standards/ilframework

Anson, Chris M., & Brown, Robert L., Jr. (1999). Subject to interpretation: The role of research in writing programs and its relationship to the politics of administration in higher education. In Shirley K Rose & Irwin Weiser (Eds.), *The writing program administrator as researcher: Inquiry in action and reflection* (pp. 141–152). Portsmouth, NH: Boynton/Cook Publishers.

Aull, Laura L., & Lancaster, Zak. (2014). Linguistic markers of stance in early and advanced academic writing: A corpus-based comparison. *Written Communication, 31*(2), 151–183.

Barton, Ellen L. (1993). Evidentials, argumentation, and epistemological stance. *College English, 55*(7), 745–769.

Beaufort, Anne. (2007). *College writing and beyond: A new framework for university writing instruction.* Logan, UT: Utah State University Press.

Bizup, Joseph. (2008). BEAM: A rhetorical vocabulary for teaching research-based writing. *Rhetoric Review, 27*(1), 72–86.

Brent, Douglass. (2013). The research paper and why we should still care. *Writing Program Administration, 37*(1), 33–53.

Broad, Bob. (2009). *Organic writing assessment: Dynamic criteria mapping in action.* Logan, UT: Utah State University Press.

Davis, Robert, & Shadle, Mark. (2000). "Building a mystery": Alternative research writing and the academic act of seeking. *College Composition and Communication, 51*(3), 417–446.

Downs, Doug, & Robertson, Liane. (2015). Threshold concepts in first-year composition. In Linda Adler-Kassner & Elizabeth A. Wardle (Eds.), *Naming what we know: Threshold concepts of writing studies* (pp. 105–121). Logan, UT: Utah State University Press.

Eodice, Michele; Geller, Anne Ellen; & Lerner, Neal. (2016). *The meaningful writing project: Learning, teaching, and writing in higher education.* https://muse.jhu.edu/book/49633

Finer, Bryna Siegel, & White-Farnham, Jamie. (2017). *Writing program architecture thirty cases for reference and research.* https://muse.jhu.edu/book/56641

Flower, Linda. (1990a). Introduction: Studying cognition in context. In Flower, Linda; Stein, Victoria; Ackerman, John; Kantz, Margaret J.; McCormick, Kathleen; & Peck, Wayne C. (Eds.), *Reading-to-write: Exploring a cognitive and social process* (pp. 3-32). New York: Oxford University Press.

Flower, Linda. (1990b). The role of task representation in reading-to-write. In Flower, Linda; Stein, Victoria; Ackerman, John; Kantz, Margaret J.; McCormick, Kathleen; & Peck, Wayne C. (Eds.), *Reading-to-write: Exploring a cognitive and social process* (pp. 35-75). New York: Oxford University Press.

Gallagher, Chris W. (2011). Being there: (Re)making the assessment scene. *College Composition and Communication, 62*(3), 450–476.

Geisler, Cheryl. (1994). *Academic literacy and the nature of expertise: Reading, writing, and knowing in academic philosophy.* Hillsdale, NJ: Lawrence Erlbaum Assoc.

Geisler, Cheryl. (2004). *Analyzing streams of language: Twelve steps to the systematic coding of text, talk, and other verbal data.* New York: Pearson/Longman.

Geisler, Cheryl. (2018). Coding for language complexity: The interplay among methodological commitments, tools, and workflow in writing research. *Written Communication, 35*(2), 215–249.

Gladstein, Jill M., & Regaignon, Dara Rossman. (2012). *Writing program administration at small liberal arts colleges.* Anderson, SC: Parlor Press.

Haller, Cynthia R. (2010). Toward rhetorical source use: Three student journeys. *Writing Program Administration, 34*(1), 33–59.

Harris, Joseph. (2017). *Rewriting: How to do things with texts* (2nd ed.). Logan, UT: Utah State University Press.

HPU Office of Research and Planning. (2018). *Fact book: 2017–2018 academic year.* http://www.highpoint.edu/researchandplanning/files/2018/01/HPU-Fact-Book-2017-2018-WEB-VERSION.pdf

Jamieson, Sandra. (2013). Reading and engaging sources: What students' use of sources reveals about advanced reading skills. *Across the Disciplines, 10*(4). http://wac.colostate.edu/atd/reading/jamieson.cfm

Jamieson, Sandra. (2017). The evolution of the Citation Project: Developing a pilot study from local to translocal. In Tricia Serviss & Sandra Jamieson (Eds.), *Points of departure: Rethinking student source use and writing studies research methods* (pp. 33–61). Logan, UT: Utah State University Press. https://muse.jhu.edu/book/57257/.

Johns, Ann M. (1997). Discourse communities and communities of practice: Membership, conflict, and diversity. In Ann M. Johns (Ed.), *Text, role, and context: developing academic literacies* (pp. 51–70). New York: Cambridge University Press.

Lancaster, Zak. (2016). Using corpus results to guide the discourse-based interview: A study of one student's awareness of stance in academic writing in philosophy. *Journal of Writing Research, 8*(1), 119–148.

Larson, Richard L. (1982). The "research paper" in the writing course: A non-form of writing. *College English, 44*(8), 811–816.

Lunsford, Karen J. (2017). Foreword. In Tricia Serviss & Sandra Jamieson (Eds.), *Points of departure: Rethinking student source use and writing studies research methods* (xiii-xx). Logan, UT: Utah State University Press. https://muse.jhu.edu/book/57257/.

Melzer, Daniel, & Zemlianksy, Pavel. (2003). Research writing in first-year composition and across the disciplines: Assignments, attitudes, and student performance. *Kairos, 8*(1).

Saldaña, Johnny. (2009). *The coding manual for qualitative researchers*. London; Thousand Oaks, CA: SAGE Publications.

Scardamalia, Marlene, & Bereiter, Carl. (1987). Knowledge telling and knowledge transforming in written composition. In Sheldon Rosenberg (Ed.), *Advances in applied psycholinguistics* (pp. 142–175). New York: Cambridge University Press.

Scheidt, Donna; Carpenter, William J.; Fitzgerald, Robert; Kozma, Cara; Middleton, Holly; & Shields, Kathy. (2017). Writing information literacy in FYC: A collaboration among faculty and librarians. In Barbara J. D'Angelo; Sandra Jamieson; Barry Maid; & Janice R. Walker (Eds.), *Information literacy: Research and collaboration across disciplines* (pp. 211–233). Fort Collins, CO; Boulder, Colorado: The WAC Clearinghouse; University Press of Colorado.

Schwegler, Robert A., & Shamoon, Linda K. (1982). The aims and process of the research paper. *College English, 44*(8), 817–824.

Serviss, Tricia. (2017). The rise of RAD research methods for writing studies: Transcontextual ways forward. In Tricia Serviss & Sandra Jamieson (Eds.), *Points of departure: Rethinking student source use and writing studies research methods* (pp. 3–22). Logan, UT: Utah State University Press. https://muse.jhu.edu/book/57257/.

Smagorinsky, Peter. (2008). The method section as conceptual epicenter in constructing social science research reports. *Written Communication, 25*(3), 389–411.

Upward Project. (2018). http://upwardproject.online/

Wardle, Elizabeth. (2009). "Mutt genres" and the goal of FYC: Can we help students write the genres of the university? *College Composition and Communication, 60*(4), 765–789.

Wolfe, Joanna; Olson, Barrie; & Wilder, Laura. (2014). Knowing what we know about writing in the disciplines: A new approach to teaching for transfer in FYC. *The WAC Journal, 25*, 42–77.

Donna Scheidt is Associate Professor of English at High Point University, specializing in rhetoric and writing studies. She launched the Upward Project, a longitudinal study of undergraduates as writer-researchers that involves research collaboration among writing faculty and librarians: https://upwardproject.online/ The project was funded with a CCCC Research Initiative grant, and she and Dr. Middleton serve as co–principal investigators.

Holly Middleton is Director of the First-Year Writing Program and Associate Professor of English at High Point University. She is a founding co-editor of *Literacy in Composition Studies* and, with Donna Scheidt, co–principal investigator of the Upward Project.

"I Know It's Going to Affect My Teaching": What Emerging Teachers Learn through Tutoring Writing

Dorothy Worden-Chambers and Amy E. Dayton

Abstract

This focus-group study followed twelve writing center tutors over the course of one academic year to examine what they learned about teaching. We captured changes in tutors' beliefs and practices over time, especially their increased empathy for students, improved interpersonal skills, and knowledge of WAC, assignment design, and ways of responding to student writing. The tutors believed their writing center experiences would shape their future teaching in positive ways. These findings suggest that WPAs and writing center directors alike may devise teacher training activities designed to help tutors transfer their pedagogical knowledge from the context of the center to that of the classroom.

Introduction

The idea that tutoring experience benefits composition teachers has wide acceptance in the discipline. For example, the CCCC Statement on Preparing Teachers of College Writing recommends writing center work as professional development for graduate TAs and instructors. Many writing programs follow this recommendation. More than half of the programs represented in Ianetta, McCamley, and Quick's study required writing center work for TA preparation (112). Even in programs that don't require writing center experience, tutoring was considered a helpful supplementary form of teacher preparation (112).

Because of their role in preparing writing teachers, both writing center directors and program administrators can benefit from a deeper understanding of what tutors learn from tutoring and how it might influence their classroom practice. Empirical investigations of tutor learning, however, are rare. Instead, arguments for the value of writing center work, while compelling, have rested primarily on anecdotal reflections by writing center directors and tutors. Few studies have examined the impact of tutoring in a systematic and data-driven way. Data-driven inquiries are needed, therefore, to test the claims of earlier studies and to identify insights not available through individual reflection alone.

Our study, relying on empirical and longitudinal data, addresses this need and adds to existing scholarship. Using focus group interviews with writing center tutors, we investigate what emerging writing teachers learn through tutoring and how they anticipate using such knowledge as they transition to the classroom. Our findings have relevance for both writing center directors and WPAs. They may help writing center directors prepare tutors to reflect on skills they have learned and prepare to transfer them into the classroom. Moreover, these findings could inform teacher preparation in programs where many instructors have previous tutoring experience, as WPAs can design training programs that build on skills that instructors have gained through one-one-one work with students.

The Role of the Writing Center in Writing Teacher Education

Existing studies of the writing center's impact on tutors, whether relying on anecdotal or empirical methods, have identified a consistent range of benefits for current and future composition teachers. One of the commonly cited ways that tutoring contributes to teachers' knowledge is through increasing their understanding of students' experiences and composing challenges. Through working with students at all stages of their writing, tutors develop a nuanced understanding of the writing process (Broder; Clark; Harris; Ianetta, McCamley, and Quick; Zelenack et al.). This awareness, in turn, can help tutors "develop sharpened diagnostic abilities" to identify students' challenges and needs, a skill they can "carry over immediately into the classroom" (Clark 348).

An increased awareness of the role and forms of writing across the curriculum (WAC) is another frequently mentioned effect of tutoring. Seeing a range of assignments, as Jackson explains, promotes a "solid grasp on the entire spectrum of academic writing and writing programs" (12). It also shows tutors what makes an assignment effective or ineffective (Clark; Harris; Ianetta, McCamley, and Quick; Zelenack et al.). Watching students work through challenging assignments helps emerging teachers to become "better prepared to create assignments that challenge and interest students after seeing what assignments work and don't" (Johnson-Schull 13). In addition to knowledge of assignment design, tutoring is frequently credited with improving confidence and skill in giving written feedback and one-on-one conferencing (Broder; Clark; Harris; Ianetta, McCamley, and Quick; Zelenak, et al.), both practical skills that translate more or less directly to the classroom.

Finally, writing center work may foster critical reflection on emerging teachers' philosophies and practices, as they learn principles of collaboration, process writing, and student-centered teaching. The non-evaluative nature of tutoring creates "a critical distance for reflection," allowing teachers "to step back and examine critically their pedagogical stances towards students," viewing them more fully as individuals (Jacobs, Danes, Jacobs, and Craig 2). In her study of ten TAs, Cogie found that tutoring had "allowed them to understand the practical implications of student-centered theory and made them significantly more committed to practicing it in the classroom" (80). These studies unanimously find that future writing teachers can develop valuable knowledge and skills through tutoring.

The value of tutoring, however, extends beyond pedagogical development. In fact, much of what tutors learn is affective and interpersonal in nature (e.g., Hughes, Gillespie, and Kail; DeFeo and Caparas; Weaver). Although our research questions focused on teacher development, we found that tutors placed equal emphasis on skills and attributes that were not explicitly pedagogical—such as self-efficacy, emotional regulation, interpersonal skills, and empathy. These abilities resemble what Driscoll has called "writing-adjacent" skills that make a critical difference in student success.

Recent scholarship has recognized the important role that emotions play in tutoring (Lawson, Evertz and Fitzpatrick) and its importance to staff training (Lape). Earlier articles—especially pedagogical pieces—treated emotion as a disruptive force, something that risked derailing a tutoring session or detracting from the *real* work of improving student writing (e.g., Devet and Barbiero; Mills). Lawson identifies this trend in a 2015 review of research, noting that scholarship on the affective dimensions of tutoring often focuses on *negative* emotion and creates a binary between emotion and logic. Lawson reminds us, however, that psychologists have found that "rather than being inherently disruptive or the opposite of reason, emotion actually plays an integral role in cognition" (25).

Emerging scholarship takes a more nuanced view of emotion, suggesting that tending to the affective dimensions of tutoring can have a positive, generative effect for tutor and learner (Yoon and Stutelberg). Moreover, surveys of former tutors reveal that they consider the development of affective knowledge, including interpersonal skills, to be a significant benefit of tutoring work (Hughes, Gillespie, and Kail; DeFeo and Caparas; Weaver).[1] Hughes, Gillespie, and Kail found that writing center work helped tutors develop skill in collaborating with others, handling "complex rhetorical situations," and active listening (27–28). The tutors in Weaver's study specifically mentioned empathy as an important skill they gained from their work (23). And DeFeo and Caparas, who followed former tutors after they

---

1. Hughes, Gillespie, and Kail note that one complication of surveying former tutors is that we can't know whether they gained skills as a result of their tutoring, or they became tutors because they already demonstrated these skills. They dealt with this potential problem by focusing on "developing" of skills rather than simply the "acquiring" of skills (18).

entered the classroom, found that they were more confident and patient with learners as a result of their time in the center. They were more likely to transfer their interpersonal knowledge to new contexts when asked to engage in reflection and analysis and to consider how they might apply this knowledge in the future.

Overall, the literature on the role of writing center work in teacher preparation is overwhelmingly positive, crediting tutoring with improving future teachers' knowledge about students, writing across the curriculum, assignment design, and feedback practices, along with affective and interpersonal skills. Yet this list of benefits is based mostly on the reflections of WC directors and former tutors rather than systematic, data-driven research or qualitative analysis. The state of knowledge of the impact of tutoring on writing teachers is much like the state of our knowledge of TA preparation overall, based more on impressions and received practices than systematic analysis, suggesting the need for "a more intensive cycle of data-driven program assessment leading to curricular and co-curricular improvements of writing pedagogy education" (Reid, Estrem, and Belcheir 62).

THE STUDY

This study responds to Reid, Estrem, and Belcheir's call for data-driven research on teacher training. It builds on the model suggested by the Peer Writing Tutor Alumni Project (Kail, Gillespie, and Hughes), which points to the importance for writing center administrators of keeping track of former staff members and gathering data about the long-term effects and benefits of tutoring on teaching and "teaching-adjacent" skills. While previous studies have relied on surveys of writing center directors and writing program administrators (Ianetta, McCamley, and Quick) or interviews and observations of former tutors (Cogie; DeFeo and Caparas; Kail et al), we were interested in the experiences of *current* tutors, especially those who planned to teach. If tutoring does benefit emergent teachers, we hoped to see evidence of this development as it happened over time. To accomplish this goal, we conducted a longitudinal, focus-group, interview-based study of twelve tutors over the course of one academic year to see what they reported learning and how they felt their knowledge would transfer into future teaching or working contexts[2].

Research Context

This study took place at a large, research-intensive university that serves as the state flagship. The writing center conducts approximately 7,000

---

2. This study was approved by the university's Office of Research Protections, IRB # 17-OR-245.

consultations per year for students at all levels and typically reaches an additional 2,000 students through events and workshops. The center employs graduate and undergraduate student tutors. Undergraduate tutors can work at the center after completing an internship course. Though many of them are English majors, some are in other disciplines, and therefore bring a wide range of knowledge about writing in the disciplines. Because our accrediting agency requires graduate students to have eighteen hours of credit before they can teach, the English Department assigns them to work as writing center tutors in their first year of post-baccalaureate study. Occasionally, more experienced TAs are assigned to the center as staffing needs fluctuate.

Participants

Tutors were approached at the first staff meeting of the year and invited to participate in the study. Twelve tutors volunteered and gave informed consent. Table 1 provides an overview of these participants.

Table 1

Study Participants

Focus Group	Tutor*	Undergrad/Grad	Program of Study	Previous WC Experience
A	Ashley	1st year GTA	TESOL**	4 years at previous institution
	George	1st year GTA	TESOL	None
	Jessie	1st year GTA	TESOL	None
	Michelle	1st year GTA	Creative Writing	1 year at previous institution
B	Erin	1st year GTA	TESOL	None
	Kendra	2nd year GTA	TESOL	1 year
	Laura	1st year GTA	Literature	None
	Lisa	1st year GTA	Creative Writing	1 year at previous institution
C	Grace	Undergrad	English major	3 years
	Mary	Undergrad	English Secondary Education major	practicum course
	Mun-Hee	Undergrad	English major	practicum course
	Natasha	Undergrad	English/Psychology major	practicum course

* Pseudonyms
**Teaching English to Speakers of Other Languages

Participants included four undergraduate tutors and nine graduate students, a proportion which reflects the overall make-up of the writing center staff.[3] The majority were starting their first semester of tutoring, though several had experience in other writing centers.[4]

Data Collection

We used focus group interviews for data collection. This format allowed us to gather insights from multiple research participants in one setting and also allowed tutors to engage in conversation that elicited their reflections on what they had learned over the course of the year. As MacNealy explains, the focus group model "is based on the assumption that the interaction of members of a small group will facilitate the uncovering of ideas that probably wouldn't surface if individuals were asked separately about their thoughts, feelings, and beliefs. . . . " (177). Good focus group research, then, is more than just an interview with multiple participants, but rather, is a "carefully planned" conversation, with participants placed in groups based on characteristics that allow for thoughtful discussion, and trained facilitators who follow specific protocols to achieve consistency across interviews and encourage interaction (177). In order to promote discussion, we formed groups of three to five participants based on tutors' status (undergraduate versus graduate) and availability. In separating undergraduate and graduate tutors, we hoped to create contexts in which participants felt comfortable sharing their thoughts with a group of peers. We varied the composition of the graduate student groups based on participants' programs of study (e.g., creative writing versus TESOL) to provide a range of disciplinary perspectives. The focus groups were facilitated by trained graduate student researchers.[5]

In order to track how tutors' knowledge and beliefs changed over time, each group was interviewed three times during the academic year. The first interview took place early in the fall semester; the second, early in the spring; and the final focus group, late in the spring semester. Prior to each interview, the facilitator reminded participants to treat the focus group as

---

3. In a typical year, we have twice as many graduate tutors as undergraduates.
4. To some extent this was a sample of convenience, because these were the students who responded to our invitation. However, MacNealy notes that a sample of convenience is not necessarily a drawback for focus group research, especially for research that intends to gather local perspectives from "in group" communities (178).
5. We used graduate student facilitators rather than faculty, so that participants would feel comfortable sharing their opinions.

a discussion rather than a formal interview and encouraged them to reply directly to one another rather than to the facilitator. Interviews began with a warm-up in which participants were asked how things were going at the writing center and invited to share stories of recent tutoring sessions they believed had contributed to their learning. At each session, we asked a few core questions based on the existing literature. These questions were designed to elicit teachers' beliefs about students, their perceptions of effective writing instruction, and their opinion regarding whether writing center work was contributing to their development. If time remained, the facilitators asked follow-up questions to spark further discussion. These questions focused on participants' beliefs about writing assignments, their feedback techniques, the rewards and challenges of tutoring, and suggestions for future tutor training and support. The same protocol and questions were repeated at each focus group to allow us to see trends and changes over time. Focus groups were recorded and transcribed.

Data Analysis

We collaboratively coded the data using grounded analysis procedures (Corbin and Strauss). Grounded theory attempts to account for the complexity of real-world research contexts by "building theory from data" rather than relying on a rigid set of codes (1). It consists of several rounds of coding that take place recursively throughout the data collection and analysis phases of a study. In the first round of coding, researchers generate an overall list of themes, while in subsequent rounds, those categories are refined and clarified (Kamberelis and Dimitriadis; Miles, Huberman, and Saldaña). Following these procedures, we created a set of twenty-four codes, then narrowed them to thirteen that illuminated the role of tutoring in teacher development (see the appendix).[6] While we were guided by our initial research questions, we remained open to themes that we did not initially anticipate.

FINDINGS

In the following section, we divide our findings into two parts, with the first being areas of learning that the tutors reported but for which we did not see significant growth or change over time. These findings broadly confirm what has been reported in previous studies of tutor learning. In the second section, we examine those elements of tutors' learning which exhibited evidence of change over the course of the study.

---

6. Once we had identified this final list of codes, both authors independently coded the data set. We then compared our codes and resolved discrepancies.

Tutors' Self-Reported Learning

In general, our study confirmed previous findings regarding the value of writing center work for teacher development. As in previous studies, our participants valued "getting to see the variety of types of writing assignments that students are required to do across the disciplines" as "one of the benefits of working in the Writing Center" (Kendra). Seeing this range of writing assignments, both successful and unsuccessful, the tutors believed, would translate to their future teaching. As Laura, explains, "I have a better understanding of how to write assignment sheets that students understand" after working in the writing center.

We found that knowledge of students' writing practices and challenges was another significant dimension of learning. The tutors valued the opportunity to work one-on-one with clients, believing that these experiences prepared them for their own classrooms. As first-year GTA Michelle explained, tutoring "gives a sample of what teaching is going to be like because you get to work with students one-on-one, so you get to see from day to day like what different problems specific students are having." This knowledge of the challenges that student writers face allowed Michelle to feel more "comfortable" and "well-informed" about her future teaching.

The tutors believed that they had learned valuable strategies for providing feedback, which they hoped to transfer to future teaching contexts. They saw feedback that was positive and clear as crucial. These beliefs arose from the experience of working with clients who were discouraged by negative or vague commentary from instructors. These experiences led the tutors to see "the importance of encouraging students" while still offering "constructive feedback" (Erin) and "being as specific and clear as possible" in their comments (Michelle).

Previous studies have shown that tutors tend to report personal growth and improved communicative abilities (writing skills, listening skills) as a result of writing center work. In general, our participants saw these skills as an important aspect of teacherly knowledge and felt that working in the Center helped them develop a stronger sense of empathy, compassion, and patience. They provided a good level of detail when discussing the interpersonal skills that they acquired during their time in the Center. As Jessie put it, working in the Center helped her learn "how to communicate on the fly . . . [if] something comes up that I'm not ready for . . . . I've learned how to handle things better on the spot." Grace noted that she had gotten better at "setting boundaries for what I can and can't do with my time" as well as

---

7. Quotes have been edited for clarity and to remove verbal fillers unrelated to the content.

listening actively, including "doing a lot of repeating back. . . . If a student is explaining something to me, then I'll rephrase it concisely and . . . [reaffirm] their understanding instead of just [saying] *does that make sense* and getting a head nod." Mary said that tutoring helped her learn how to give "bad news," especially for students whose papers needed significant revision. She said, "I used to be really bad at giving bad news," but over time she learned to "do that in a way that students aren't frustrated . . . not so much saying, 'this is a bad paragraph, you need to rewrite it, [but] pointing to the good things that a paragraph has and then [pointing out] what you can redo." Tutors considered these skills not only professionally valuable but relevant to their personal lives. As George put it, "some of the communicative skills are things that will help personal, everyday life . . . it's a lifelong journey of learning those things, but becoming a confident communicator is going to help, not just as a teacher. Things like listening, patience, adaptability are going to help you."

One unanticipated interview theme was student identity and voice. Tutors often mentioned their desire to help students' preserve their own voice and their concern that academic writing makes students feel pressured to write in a voice that is not their own. As Grace said, "students think that they need to put on this academic mask in their writing, and they need to use all these *therefores* and *whatnots* and *thus* and *furthermore*, which is good, but in the process they've lost their personality and their own personal style . . . so I think pointing out . . . places where they can maintain personal style and still have an academic writing style has become important."

The tutors recognized this conflict as a site of tension, especially for multilingual writers. Erin noted that her linguistics coursework made her think differently about the relationship between language and culture, especially for students who write with an "accent." Kendra noted that this tension was especially acute for international graduate students, who are preparing articles for publication: "you want to help preserve their voice, but at the same time you understand that when they submit this for publication, if it's written in a voice that doesn't seem like it's a native English speaker, it's probably going to be kicked back to them . . . so it's challenging." Building on Kendra's comments, Erin remarked that "it's right for people to be able to speak with their own voice. We're battling this external world . . . of this is right and this is wrong and everything needs to sound like a native speaker of English, but in reality that will never happen . . . the Writing Center showed me the struggle of letting students feel valued and speak in their own voice. But then, how do we help them not get a really bad grade?"

The tutors didn't offer definitive solutions for helping students preserve their own voice. And to be fair, seasoned scholars continue to debate the best methods for helping students preserve their cultural and linguistic identities in their writing. But working in the Center has clearly given tutors first-hand experience with this issue and illustrated its complexities.

Evidence for Tutor Development Over Time

Our longitudinal approach allowed us to capture changes in tutors' thinking over time. In the following sections, we examine dimensions of tutor learning for which we saw evidence of change.

Recognizing the complexity of tutoring and teaching. One change we observed as the tutors moved through the year was an increased sensitivity to the complexities of tutoring and teaching writing. When asked what constitutes effective writing instruction, what challenges student writers face, and what kinds of feedback benefit students most, the tutors frequently responded with a variation of "it depends." For some, this growing awareness of the contingent nature of writing instruction was one of the biggest changes in their knowledge and practice during the year.

For example, Mary, an undergraduate tutor planning to teach high school English, showed a clear change in her orientation to tutoring, and by extension teaching, as the year progressed. In the first focus group, Mary, as a new tutor, described how she had struggled with "setting the agenda" with clients but was now "settling into the groove. I know my system now . . . focus on the higher order and then lower order." The "groove" and "system" Mary relied upon helped her develop confidence. Yet in the second focus group, Mary began to question the utility of her "system." She explained that "One of the things I noticed last semester is that . . . I tried to use the same structure for each of my appointments, and that is not something that's really feasible because every appointment is different. Every client is different." This developing awareness that a one-size-fits all approach was not realistic given the diversity of students led Mary to begin to "trust the students' worries" about their own writing and to "focus more on that [students' concerns] than what I think is important."

In the final focus group, Mary built on this previous realization, noting that "we need to meet students where they're at . . . we need to meet them at their understanding and then develop from there." Though similar to her comments in the second focus group, this final version demonstrates an increased level of abstraction. Rather than simply focusing on how to structure a consultation, she expresses a developing philosophy of teaching writing—one that extends beyond the context of writing center consultation and can be adapted to future teaching.

Another example of this understanding of the contingent nature of writing instruction is evinced by Laura, a first-year GTA studying literature. In the first focus group, Laura noted her surprise that the students she was tutoring "don't understand they have creative control of their papers" to incorporate their own cultures and voices. This observation led Laura to try "to encourage students" and to "empower their voice in their papers" through her tutoring practice. In the final focus group, however, Laura brought new levels of nuance to her discussion of the role of student agency and voice. In reflecting on her learning over the year, Laura reported that:

Over time I've come to kind of understand even though it's their creative process, and you can empower them to write it however they want to write it, there's also times where they just need someone to be like, "No, you can do it this way and it will work."

Here, while Laura still holds to her original belief that "writing is a creative process" and that she can "empower" students to approach a project in their own way, she acknowledges that this strategy is not always effective; there are times when students need a directive approach. This new awareness is not a rejection of her earlier position, but an acknowledgement that any principle or value in writing instruction is subject to situation and context. This contextualization, we argue, is a crucial awareness for developing teachers.

Personalizing and empathizing with student writers. For most tutors, working in the Center improved their understanding of students' challenges and needs, and personalized their approach to teaching. Ken Bain, who conducted a longitudinal study of the most effective postsecondary instructors, notes that the best college teachers are those who "take their students seriously as human beings" and show interest in "students' lives, cultures, and aspirations" (145). It seemed to us that working on-one-one with writing center clients helped the tutors begin thinking of students in these terms. Erin, for example, explained that working in the center had taught her "to focus on [clients] and see them as individuals, so that when I am a teacher and I don't just have one student, but I have many more that . . . I am able to focus on them as an individual . . . and not just see [them] as this mass of students."

Closely related to seeing students as individuals was empathizing with them as writers and as people. The tutors frequently spoke about frustrations as writers, which mirrored their clients' difficulties. For instance, discussing how clients struggled to focus on higher order concerns when faced with a detailed assignment sheet, Mun-Hee said, "I really sympathize with that 'cause when I have a writing assignment I go for something that's easy first." Beyond just empathizing with clients' writing challenges, interacting with students one-on-one gave the tutors a richer picture of students' socioacademic lives. Kendra, for instance, emphasized that student writers' challenges were not only related to writing, but to issues like "adjusting to campus life" and the anxiety and "fear going into that first college assignment." This awareness of students as individuals with challenges that the tutors could empathize with was one of the most frequently reported benefits of writing center work.

Looking at the longitudinal data offers us a unique perspective on how tutor learning developed throughout the year. For example, Lisa, a first-year GTA working toward her MFA in creative writing, experienced a change in her relationship with and attitude toward students through the course of her tutoring. While Lisa was never negative about students and, indeed, from the beginning sought to believe the best about them, she struggled to connect and empathize with clients at the beginning of the year. This was partly because Lisa tutored mostly online. Being physically removed from the students, she explained, "I can't sit with the student and watch them have their ah-ha moment or hear their responses to the question that I ask." This distance was "the biggest challenge" of the format and resulted in Lisa believing that "I have a lot more difficulty understanding where a student is coming from and empathizing with them. . . . It's really easy to become frustrated and just sit there in front of the computer and say things to myself like 'My god, how did you get into college?', which is not the mindset I want to bring to working with students." Though Lisa clearly knows that an understanding mindset is more productive, cultivating and sustaining empathy while tutoring online initially proved difficult.

In her second semester, Lisa switched to face-to-face tutoring, a change that helped her better relate to students. In fact, in the second focus group, when asked, "What is one thing you learned from working in the writing center that was a surprise to you?," she responded, "I like students. Most of them arrive with goodwill rather than recalcitrance." In comparison to her first focus group where she had the desire and drive to connect with students but struggled to do so, this simple sentiment of "I like students" signals a positive change. This change may have resulted from switching to face-to-face tutoring, or from having simply acquired additional experience. Regardless of the reason, this new attitude toward students was the primary thing Lisa hoped to carry into her future teaching, saying that "When I'm set loose with my own students next semester, I hope I will remember this experience and treat them with the respect they deserve."

Another tutor, Mun-Hee, made a transition over the course of the academic year from a self-focused to a student-centered approach to tutoring. In her first interview, Mun-Hee described anxiety over her own writing skills, which she perceived to be lacking: "It's so painful," she said, "because I go back to my own writing sometimes . . . and I feel like, are you kidding, you're at this level and you mean to actually tutor somebody?" When asked to describe a challenging session, she described a consultation with a "bulky guy from a fraternity" who didn't seem responsive to her feedback. This consultation caused her to reflect on her positionality in relation to students: "It was probably . . . my pre-established bias and his physicality... and a little bit of defensive behavior" that derailed the session. "I felt at times self-conscious because I am of different race," Mun-Hee said, expressing her worry that both American and Asian students might respond differently to her because she is Korean.

In this early interview, we see Mun-Hee beginning to work through her anxieties about her ability and biases toward students. In a follow-up interview, she noted: "Last semester I was too busy being scared of students; I didn't notice that students coming to the writing center are scared." She began focusing on caring for the anxious students instead of focusing on her own fears: "I should handle their feelings carefully because their writing is their expression and it contains a lot of their feelings. I need to handle that with care." Mun-Hee remarked with surprise that some of her earlier fears turned out to be "stupid worries" because she discovered that "[students] really trust me." She moved from being anxious about her own writing to showing an increased desire to alleviate student anxiety. Like Mun-Hee, many of our participants reported that tutoring experience helped them view students through a more humane, empathetic lens, recognize and address students' affective needs, and better understand how students' affective responses shaped their ability to collaborate and learn.

Developing a philosophy for teaching writing. A common theme among all the previous sections is the tutors' active reflection on their beliefs about writing instruction and their developing identities as teachers. In other words, the tutors were not only acquiring discrete facts and practices but were beginning to develop a coherent teaching philosophy. This development can be seen in Mary's growing awareness of the complexity and contingency of writing instruction and in Mun-Hee's desire to attend to students' emotional needs. For the majority, their developing teaching philosophies emphasized the affective domains of teaching and learning. For example, the question "what do you think of as good writing instruction?" routinely yielded responses such as "good writing instruction should be compassionate and take into consideration the very real challenges and fears that a lot of students face" (Kendra); "good writing instruction is as personal as possible. It is empathetic" (Lisa); and "it just starts with a lot of respect" (Michelle).

Many tutors' developing teaching philosophies incorporated not only their experiences in the writing center, but also their identities outside of it. Kendra, for example, attributed her beliefs about compassionate instruction to her "personal values that consider people as valuable and as worth investing in." For some, the writing center assisted them in incorporating their values into their teaching persona. For example, George, a first-year GTA in the TESOL program, noted in the first focus group that working in the writing center sparked "a shift in my own attitude towards writing and my own attitude towards teaching." This shift, George went on to explain, built on his perception of himself as "someone who's celebratory, [who] want[s] to celebrate things in other people's lives." As he began working in the writing center, George started to apply this celebratory ethic to his clients and believed "that as a teacher someday, that's something that I want to apply to my students." For George, this philosophy of celebrating students' accomplishments wove together his values outside of academia with his growing awareness of the emotional stakes of writing, prompting him to give encouraging feedback to his clients. Such findings support arguments by Jacobs, Danes, Jacobs, and Craig that the writing center provides a valuable space for teachers to reflect on their philosophies and practices. The non-evaluative nature of tutoring, along with the interpersonal negotiation of working one-on-one seems to have helped these tutors develop not only valuable practices, but also a teacher identity that integrates their sense of themselves as ethical and emotionally intelligent people.

Discussion

Our study confirms previous findings that writing center work does contribute to the professional development of preservice teachers (Broder; Clark; Harris; Ianetta, McCamley, and Quick; Zelenack et al.). Based on our interviews, it seems clear that tutoring imparts skills that emerging teachers can use in future classrooms. While some aspects of teaching (lesson planning, curriculum design) do not arise in a tutoring context, many other dimensions of teaching and learning do play out in the one-on-one writing center environment.

Beyond the benefits noted by other researchers, our study highlighted dimensions of tutors' development that dealt with their understanding of voice and identity in writing, particularly for linguistically and culturally marginalized students. The tutors in our study not only demonstrated increased knowledge of linguistic issues, but, more importantly, were engaged with the complex relationships of language, culture, identity, and faculty expectations. Given the resilient nature of teachers' standard language ideologies (Schreiber and Worden), the complexity and sensitivity of the tutors' positions on student language is encouraging. The fact that these discussions took place among peers, rather than in the presence of a supervisor, suggests honest questioning and growth on tutors' part. Their interest in this issue, and commitment to helping students' preserve their own voice, suggests the benefits of training that invites tutors and writers to negotiate the "contact zone" between academic English and students' home languages and discourses (Pratt). Although the tutors may not have theoretical knowledge regarding students' right to their own language (SRTOL) or translingual pedagogies, their discussion of student voice shows that they recognize the importance to students of composing texts that will help them meet their academic goals without sacrificing their cultural or linguistic identity (Horner, Lu, Royster, and Trimbur; National Council of Teachers of English).

Our interviewees demonstrated a significant focus on the affective domains of tutoring and teaching. While previous studies have acknowledged the importance of tutor and client emotion (Hughes, Gillespie, and Kail; DeFeo and Caparas; Weaver) most discussions have treated the emotional dimensions of tutoring as distinct from the cognitive (Lawson). For our tutors, however, these dimensions were deeply intertwined. Their empathy and awareness of student emotion, for example, were not separate from their knowledge of students' writing challenges. In fact, when asked what they had learned from the writing center that they would carry into teaching, the majority of responses focused on emotion, be confident, care about students, respect students, treat students with kindness.

An additional contribution of our study comes from its longitudinal nature. By following tutors for a year, we saw their growth over time. This growth seemed especially apparent in graduate students—perhaps because they anticipated entering the classroom soon, while for undergraduate participants, future teaching was farther away (if indeed they planned on teaching). The graduate students even talked about the fact that they were encountering the *same* students, in the *same* classes, that they would teach the following fall.

We noticed changes over time even in cases where tutors did not perceive a change (after all, they did not have access to their transcripts over time, as we did). At the end of the year, several students, including Mun-Hee and Mary, told us their ideas "didn't change much" (Mun-Hee) or "I do not think my beliefs have changed" (Mary). Because tutors' self-perception sometimes varies from what we see in their transcripts, it may be that qualitative interviews are a more effective means of tracking tutor development than surveys or single interviews, which don't show change over time.

Finally, it is important to note the role that the focus groups themselves played in not only capturing but also promoting tutor development. Being asked to reflect on their tutoring could spark changes that otherwise might not have been as marked; in other words, the study itself may have resulted in growth. In their study of tutor development, Defeo and Caparas note that "Although the tutors' comments about their tutoring processes yielded sentiments and realizations that would make any writing center administrator proud, it is unclear whether they reflected on their experiences and made these connections independently, or whether the phenomenological reflective process is itself (at least in part) responsible for their ability to make these connections in retrospect" (156). Studies like theirs and ours suggest the benefits of reflection for emerging teachers.

As teacher and tutor educators ourselves, we find these results both enlightening and encouraging. Still, our study has limitations, which could be addressed in future research. One limitation is the relatively sparse information we collected regarding our participants' past and concurrent experiences with writing, tutoring, and teaching. While we collected demographic information such as area of study and years of previous teaching experience, and while our participants occasionally volunteered information about experiences outside of the center that contributed to their learning, we did not conduct systematic interviews with each participant about their backgrounds. As a result, we have little insight regarding how past experiences such as previous tutoring, academic coursework, or their own writing education shaped their learning. Given the diverse experiences and training of tutors, this is perhaps particularly important. Future research could address this limitation by collecting more extensive background information from each participant. Such data, whether in the form of surveys or interviews, would allow researchers to account for the range of experiences in and outside the writing center that contribute to tutor development.

Similarly, while our study provided evidence that tutors' knowledge developed over the course of the study, these self-reports are not direct evidence of tutor improvement or benefit to students. Moreover, we do not know if the knowledge and practices tutors intended to utilize in their future teaching will indeed transfer to the classroom. Future research could incorporate direct observations of tutoring sessions. Extending the length of the study would allow researchers to follow tutors into the classroom, providing evidence of the impact of tutoring on their pedagogical practice.

Future researchers may want to look more closely into tutors' understanding of voice in relation to SRTOL, both for native and non-native speakers (Canagarajah; Canagarajah and Matsumoto; Shafer). Tutors' discussions of international students' struggles, for instance, suggested their awareness that cultural and vernacular differences in writing can be assets rather than detriments, yet at the same time, these aspects of writing are often singled out for remediation by faculty members. The tutors' interest in students' voice and in language variation raises questions for writing center administration: are tutors learning about these issues as part of their training? How do tutors' language attitudes shape their decisions in working with students from a range of language backgrounds? As these topics and issues become established parts of writing center theory, more research will be needed to understand how they play out on the ground level (Fitzgerald and Ianetta).

Conclusion

As emerging teachers transition from tutoring to teaching, reflection is an important tool, as Weaver argues, which can help tutors "more consciously transfer knowledge" (23). Both writing center directors and writing program administrators can promote reflection and transfer. Writing center directors, for example, might include opportunities for tutors to discuss what they are learning in the writing center and consider how it might apply to future teaching, as part of their professional development. Once tutors become classroom teachers, WPAs can play an important role in fostering reflection on how skills developed in the writing center can be transferred to classroom teaching.

Reflection while teaching may be of particular importance. The tutors in our study were not always sure how tutoring might contribute to their future teaching, though they believed it would. Michelle, for example, noticed that though she had been actively reflecting on how to translate her tutoring experiences to the classroom, "I'm still not really sure how to do that, but it's something that I've been trying to process and figure out." Jessie concurred, saying "I know it's going to affect my teaching," although identifying these effects would "take reflection" and "me actually being in the classroom and just seeing it once I'm doing it." By providing opportunities for reflection (including group reflections similar to the focus groups), WPAs can help ensure that the beliefs and practices tutors gain do indeed impact their classroom practice.

Of course, we have not yet followed tutors into the classroom to track how the skills they discussed in the study show up in their classroom.

However, our focus groups did make clear that they had acquired new skills, developed complex ideas about writing and teaching, formed personal, empathetic relationships with their clients, and begun to see themselves as seasoned, competent professionals with much to offer.

Works Cited

Bain, Ken. *What the Best College Teachers Do*. Harvard UP, 2004.

Broder, Peggy F. "Writing Centers and Teacher Training." *WPA: Writing Program Administration*, vol. 13, no. 3, 1990, p. 5.

Canagarajah, A. Suresh. "'Blessed in My Own Way:' Pedagogical Affordances for Dialogical Voice Construction in Multilingual Student Writing." *Journal of Second Language Writing*, vol. 27, Mar. 2015, pp. 122–39. *DOI.org (Crossref)*, doi:10.1016/j.jslw.2014.09.001.

Canagarajah, Suresh, and Yumi Matsumoto. "Negotiating Voice in Translingual Literacies: From Literacy Regimes to Contact Zones." *Journal of Multilingual and Multicultural Development*, vol. 38, no. 5, May 2017, pp. 390–406. *DOI.org (Crossref)*, doi:10.1080/01434632.2016.1186677.

Clark, Irene Lurkis. "Preparing Future Composition Teachers in the Writing Center." *College Composition and Communication*, vol. 39, no. 3, 1988, pp. 347–50. http://www.jstor.org/stable/357473. Accessed 6 Sept. 2021.

Cogie, Jane. "Theory Made Visible: How Tutoring May Effect Development of Student-Centered Teachers." *WPA: Writing Program Administration*, vol. 21, no. 1, 1997, pp. 76–85.

CCCC Statement on Preparing Teachers of College Writing. CCCC, 2015, https://cccc.ncte.org/cccc/resources/positions/statementonprep. Accessed 6 Sept. 2021.

Corbin, Juliet, and Anselm Strauss. *Basics of Qualitative Research: Techniques and Procedures for Developing Grounded Theory*. 3rd ed., SAGE Publications, Inc, 2012.

DeFeo, Dayna Jean, and Fawn Caparas. "Tutoring as Transformative Work: A Phenomenological Case Study of Tutors' Experiences." *Journal of College Reading and Learning*, vol. 44, no. 2, Apr. 2014, pp. 141–63. *Crossref*, doi:10.1080/10790195.2014.906272.

Devet, Bonnie, and Alison Barbiero. "Dear Labby: Stressing Interpersonal Relationships in a Writing Center." *The Writing Lab Newsletter* vol. 36, no. 5–6, 2012, pp. 11–13.

Driscoll, Dana. "Come Here, and You Will Grow: Connecting Writing Development with Writing Center Practices." Southeastern Writing Centers Association. February 21, 2020, University of Alabama-Birmingham. Keynote speech.

Evertz, Kathy, and Fitzpatrick, Renata. *The Writing Lab Newsletter* [special issue]. May/June 2018.

Fitzgerald, Lauren, and Melissa Ianetta. "Tutor and Writer Identities." *The Oxford Guide for Writing Tutors: Practice and Research*. Oxford UP, 2016.

Harris, Muriel. "'What Would You Like to Work on Today?': The Writing Center as a Site for Teacher Training." *Preparing College Teachers of Writing*, edited by Betty P. Pytlik and Sarah Liggett, Oxford UP, 2002, pp. 194–207.

Horner, Bruce, Min-Zhan Lu, Jacqueline Jones Royster, and John Trimbur. "Language Difference in Writing: Toward a Translingual Approach." *College English*, vol. 73, no. 3, 2011, pp. 303–21.

Hughes, Bradley, Paula Gillespie, and Harvey Kail. "What They Take with Them: Findings from the Peer Writing Tutor Alumni Research Project." *The Writing Center Journal*, vol. 30, no. 2, 2010, pp. 12–46. *JSTOR*, https://www.jstor.org/stable/43442343. Accessed 6 September 2021.

Ianetta, Melissa, Michael McCamley, and Catherine Quick. "Taking Stock: Surveying the Relationship of the Writing Center and TA Training." *WPA: Writing Program Administration*, vol. 31, no. 1–2, 2007, pp. 104–124.

Jackson, Alan. "Writing Centers: A Panorama to Teaching and the Profession." *Writing Lab Newsletter*, vol 18, no. 6, 1994, pp. 1–2, 12.

Jacobs, Dale, Jennifer Bradley Danes, Heidi Jacobs and Chauna Craig. "Evolving Pedagogies: Four Voices on Teacher Change and the Writing Center." *Writing Lab Newsletter* vol. 22, no. 10, 1998, pp. 1–9.

Johnson-Schull, Lisa. "Teaching Assistants Learn Teaching Tips by Tutoring." *Writing Lab Newsletter*, vol. 18, no. 9, 1994, p. 13.

Kail, Harvey, Paula Gillespie and Bradley Hughes. *Peer Writing Tutor Alumni Research Project*. University of Wisconsin, https://writing.wisc.edu/peer-writing-tutor-alumni-research-project/. Accessed 6 Sept. 2021.

Kamberelis, George, and Greg Dimitriadis. *Qualitative Inquiry: Approaches to Language and Literacy Research*. Teachers College P, 2005.

Lape, Noreen. "Training Tutors in Emotional Intelligence: Toward a Pedagogy of Empathy." *Writing Lab Newsletter* vol. 33, no. 2, 2008, pp. 1–6.

Lawson, Daniel. "Metaphors and Ambivalence: Affective Dimensions in Writing Center Studies." *WLN: A Journal of Writing Center Scholarship*, vol. 40, no. 3–4, 2015, pp. 20–27.

MacNealy, Mary Sue. *Strategies for Empirical Research in Writing*. Needham Heights, MA: Allyn & Bacon, 1999.

Miles, Matthew B., A. Michael Huberman and Johnny Saldaña. *Qualitative Data Analysis: A Methods Sourcebook*. Third edition, SAGE Publications, Inc, 2014.

Mills, Gayla. "Preparing for Emotional Sessions." *The Writing Lab Newsletter* vol. 35, no. 5–6, 2011, pp. 1–5.

National Council of Teachers of English. "Resolution on Affirming the CCCC "Students' Right to Their Own Language." 2003 NCTE Annual Business Meeting in San Francisco, California. November 3, 2003. http://ncte.org/statement/affirmingstudents/. Accessed 6 Sept. 2021.

Pratt, Mary Louise. "Arts of the Contact Zone." *Profession* 1991, pp. 33–40.

Reid, E. Shelley, Heidi Estrem and Marcia Belcheir. "The Effects of Writing Pedagogy Education on Graduate Teaching Assistants' Approaches to Teaching Composition." *WPA: Writing Program Administration*, vol. 36, no. 1, 2012, pp. 32–73.

Schreiber, Brooke Ricker, and Dorothy Worden. "'Nameless, Faceless People': How Other Teachers' Expectations Influence Our Pedagogy." *Composition Studies*, vol. 47, no. 1, 2019, pp. 57–72.

Shafer, Gregory. "Negotiating Audience and Voice in the Writing Center." *Teaching English in the Two-Year College*, vol. 27, no. 2, 1999, pp. 220–28.

Weaver, Brent. "Is Knowledge Repurposed from Tutoring to Teaching? A Qualitative Study of Transfer from the Writing Center." *Writing Lab Newsletter*, vol. 43, no. 1–2, 2018, pp. 1824. https://wlnjournal.org/archives/v43/43.1-2.pdf. Accessed 6 Sept. 2021.

Yoon, Stephanie Rollag, and Erin B. Stutelberg. "The Generative Power of Affect in a High School Writing Center." *Writing Lab Newsletter* vol. 42, no. 9–10, 2018, pp. 18–25.

Zelenak, Bonnie, Irv Cockriel, Eric Crump and Elaine Hocks. "Ideas in Practice: Preparing Composition Teachers in the Writing Center." *Journal of Developmental Education*, vol. 17, no. 1, Fall 1993, pp. 28–30, 32, 34. Stable URL: http://www.jstor.org/stable/42774628. Accessed 6 Sept. 2021.

Appendix: List of Codes

Knowledge and Beliefs
Good Writing
Good Writing Instruction
Perceptions of WAC
Perceptions of Students

Affective and Interpersonal
Embodiment
Empathy
Interpersonal Skills
Tutor Emotion (positive)
Tutor Emotion (negative)

Tutor Reflection
Future Teaching
Source of knowledge (or belief)
Tutor growth (writing center)
Tutor growth (non-writing center)

Dorothy Worden-Chambers is Assistant Professor at The University of Alabama. Her research examining the development of teachers of second language writing has recently appeared in *The Journal of Second Language Writing*, *Composition Forum*, and *Teacher Development*.

Amy E. Dayton is Associate Professor and Director of the Writing Center at The University of Alabama. Her recent work includes two collections, *Assessing the Teaching of Writing* (University of Colorado/Utah State University Press), and the new volume, *Ethics and Representation in Feminist Rhetorical Inquiry* (University of Pittsburgh Press).

The Laborious Reality vs. the Imagined Ideal of Graduate Student Instructors of Writing

Ruth Osorio, Allison Hutchison, Sarah Primeau, Molly E. Ubbesen, and Alexander Champoux-Crowley

ABSTRACT

In fall 2017, the Writing Program Administration Graduate Organization (WPA-GO) Labor Census Task Force surveyed 344 graduate student instructors (GSIs) of writing from across the U.S. about their labor conditions. Our findings highlight the material challenges GSIs face in writing programs: low pay, inconsistent access to healthcare, and little support for health and family life. These labor conditions, we argue, construct an imagined ideal GSI, disproportionately impacting GSIs with marginalized identities.

DEDICATION

This article is dedicated to Katie McWain, an early enthusiastic member of the WPA-GO Labor Census Task Force.

INTRODUCTION

Graduate student instructors (GSIs) occupy a complex, contested role in writing programs. Within writing programs, graduate students from various disciplines will often be the instructor of record who designs syllabi, crafts assignments and lesson plans, and assesses student writing. This labor is crucial to institutions of higher education across the United States. According to the 2014 MLA Survey of Departmental Staffing, GSIs make up the majority of the composition writing instructional faculty at PhD-granting institutions (nearly 40%) and a considerable proportion at MA-granting institutions (15%). Despite the fact that GSIs largely fuel the work of writing programs, the labor of GSIs is often overlooked as labor. GSIs are framed as students first, apprentices second, and workers rarely. This framing has led to a dearth of data on the labor conditions of GSIs in writing programs, a gap we aimed to examine in a nation-wide survey in 2017[1]. 344 GSIs reported information about their stipends, healthcare, leave policies, teaching load, and other labor conditions. Our survey questions can be found here: https://bit.ly/GSIsurveydata. In this article, we expand on the information in our 2019 "Report on Graduate Student Instructor

Labor Conditions in Writing Programs" (https://bit.ly/GSIsurveydata) and overtly argue for more humane treatment of GSIs in writing programs.

Our findings highlight the material challenges GSIs face in writing programs, including low pay, inconsistent access to healthcare, and little support for mental health and family life. Through our analysis of survey data, we advance two claims. First, universities, graduate programs, and writing programs must ensure humane labor conditions for GSIs. Recent literature suggests this approach has pragmatic benefits such that improving the labor conditions of teachers leads to improved student outcomes (Barnum, 2016). More importantly, we want to work in a profession that fairly compensates all ranks of labor because it is the just and equitable thing to do. Second, a lack of humane labor conditions contributes to a lack of diversity in the profession. The typical working conditions of GSIs, we argue, paint a picture of academia's *imagined ideal*, a term we use to describe a graduate student who has outside financial support and who never gets sick or disabled or has children. Inadequate stipends and healthcare coverage pose a challenge for many potential and current GSIs and may pose a greater challenge still for GSIs from marginalized communities, such as non-white, working class, queer, and/or disabled GSIs. For writing studies to become a more diverse field, we must fiercely advocate for more humane labor practices that address the needs of GSIs from underrepresented communities.

Tracing the GSI-as-Worker in Writing Studies and Beyond

Composition courses occupy a paradoxical role in the university, at once in demand and undervalued. These courses are deemed essential, often required for incoming students. At the same time, composition courses are often framed as a service course rather than a rich site of knowledge making. Writing studies scholars have argued that the evidence of the university's disdain for composition can be seen in increasing casualization of writing faculty: the phenomenon of long-term permanent positions turning into short-term precarious positions (Crowley, 1998; Kahn et al., 2017). As Kirsti Cole (2019) explains, "the increased demand for, and location of, standing composition programs at colleges and universities required a cheap labor solution to fill the need gap created by the enrollment increases" (p. 155). We posit that the work of teaching composition and the labor of GSIs are both still undervalued in the university, compounding in multiple layers of exploitation that perpetuates the overall casualization of writing faculty (Samuels, 2017, p. 16). Robert Samuels (2017) argues the increasing presence of GSIs in writing classes is one of the reasons "there are so few jobs for graduate students after they earn their PhDs" (16). By depending heavily on graduate labor, writing programs, especially at research universities, can avoid hiring full-time faculty to teach first-year writing.

Graduate students' historical role of easy, cheap labor in the writing class highlights their paradoxical role in a writing program: both student and faculty, apprentice *and* instructor of record. As Michael Bérubé (2013) wryly notes, the apprenticeship model "dates back to the days of the guilds, [when] the apprentices got jobs" (n.p.). If grad students are not guaranteed jobs after graduation, what is a graduate assistantship preparation for? Marc Bousquet (2002) asserts that graduate school is not preparation for a teaching career, but rather, the start and end of most teaching careers (p. 88). Scholars such as Bérubé and Bousquet reveal an uncomfortable truth: graduate student teaching is rarely *preparation* for a stable teaching career. And yet, despite the critiques of the apprenticeship model as outdated, it continues to haunt graduate education—leading to wide-ranging material impacts. As Allison Laubach Wright (2017) asserts, "when it prevents new thinking about a broken system and silences dissent for exploitative labor situations, maintaining the language of the apprenticeship model is directly implicated in the larger problems of the labor system" (pp. 275-276). Wright's critique of the apprenticeship model is echoed in graduate labor organizing, in particular, efforts to unionize. Roxanne Mountford (2002) observes, "that the work of a GTA is work—not a kind of apprenticeship for which universities can award poverty-level wages—has been underscored by the efforts of graduate students to unionize nationwide" (p. 43). Indeed, apprentices lack access to the benefits of employment, with legal protections for collective bargaining, the Family and Medical Leave Act (FMLA), and long-term disability not extending to GSIs.

The increased casualization of writing instruction, emboldened by the apprenticeship model of graduate labor, creates an imagined ideal writing teacher that is both raced and gendered. The work of teaching writing has historically been framed as white women's work. Donna Strickland (2011) notes this trend emerged in the early twentieth century when white women were relegated to "the lowest levels of the academic hierarchy while simultaneously elevating the primarily white, native-born, teachers as keepers of correctness and racial propriety" (p. 38). Strickland's historical analysis illustrates the emergence of the imagined ideal writing teacher: a woman, as the work of teaching writing is associated with secretarial work rather than the work of big ideas, and a white woman, as the job entails maintaining racial propriety through surveillance and assessment of student writing. Thus, feminization of composition instruction justified the poor labor conditions for writing faculty, while at the same time, the racialization of composition instruction justified the exclusion of non-white bodies. These associations were not left behind in the twentieth century. Recently, Eileen Schell (2017) posed the following questions:

> how is contingency tied to the bodies of workers and students that are marked as non-normative and different? In a globalized economy, white women, women of color, and men of color, working class men and women, people living with disabilities, and queer and trans people are often treated as an exploitable and expendable workforce; how does higher education mirror that exploitation? (pp. xiv-xv)

Schell's questions prompt us to consider how hierarchies of acceptable bodies continue to dictate labor conditions. Contingency is not only relevant to adjunct labor but also to GSIs, as their positions are contingent on their progress through graduate education. Liminality, too, is tied to certain bodies. How are the non-normative bodies Schell names stuck in-between ranks: never fully faculty, never fully student, never fully protected as employees?

Our study attempts to bring together conversations about the undervaluing of composition, graduate labor, and non-normative bodies, and illustrates how this layered undervaluing has compounded to create an untenable situation for many GSIs, especially those from underrepresented communities. As Laura Colaneri (2019), a graduate student organizer, insists, "bettering working conditions and increasing wages through a union can only serve to make graduate school more accessible to marginalized groups" (n.p.). Colaneri and other GSI organizers highlight how poor conditions threaten the ability of GSIs from underrepresented communities to complete their degrees as well as the unpaid diversity work often heaped upon graduate workers of color (Kesslen, 2019; Watlington, 2019). Colaneri, Strickland, Schell, and Bousquet insist that labor conditions welcome or forbid certain bodies. Our data below paints a picture of low stipends, overwhelming workloads, inadequate health care, and vague parental/medical leave policies that imagine an ideal GSI. Particularly in the moments where the demographics of participants in our survey seemed to echo this ideal, we hope to highlight the struggles of the participants who did NOT fit this imagined ideal—people of color, disabled people, queer folks, parents, and/or working-class scholars. The labor conditions we explore present a barrier to entry into the professoriate for these GSIs.

Surveying GSIs

In early 2017, the newly formed WPA-GO Labor Census Task Force began to develop a survey to understand the working conditions of GSIs. Like Sarah Liggett, Kerri Jordan, and Steve Price (2011), we see that surveys are both method and inquiry, and as such, function *"methodologically* as a distinctive way of making knowledge" (p. 68). Liggett, Jordan, and Price offer the example of Jo Ann Griffin et al.'s 2007 article reporting survey data from the Writing Centers Research Project (WCRP) in order to demonstrate that the focus is not only on numbers, but "the survey responses also create a nationwide mosaic of how writing centers operate" (p. 67). Following these scholars, we sought to illustrate the mosaic of graduate students' experiences, starting with the research question: How do labor conditions within graduate writing programs operate and how do GSIs experience those conditions?

We hypothesized that asking GSIs to evaluate the adequacy of their stipends and healthcare benefits would help us understand how these labor conditions precondition and give rise to the situation at hand. Like Cristyn L. Elder, Megan Schoen, and Ryan Skinnell (2014), we attempted to gather large-scale survey data about GSIs' lived experience. We worked toward this objective with sixteen multi-point questions with yes/no, multiple choice, and open-ended responses on stipends, workload, healthcare benefits, leave policies and the experiential dimensions of those conditions. We wanted to amplify the perceptions and experiences of GSIs to explore how the mosaic of their labor conditions contributes to the imagined ideal GSI.

After obtaining IRB approval and conducting usability testing, we moved on to survey distribution in late September 2017. We recruited participants using multiple and redundant strategies to access a variety of institutional contexts. Through a process of distributed snowball sampling, we circulated the survey via social media (Facebook, Twitter, Instagram), email listservs (WPA-L, WPA-GO), and emails to DGSs and WPAs at institutions listed in the Consortium of Doctoral Programs in Rhetoric and Composition and The Master's Consortium of Writing Studies Specialists, asking them to forward our survey link to their GSIs.

Data Analysis

While most questions resulted in quantitative data, five open-ended questions and demographic questions afforded for more qualitative responses that required coding. To code responses to "other" and open-ended questions, we used qualitative data analysis methods (Creswell, 2014). For each qualitative survey response item, two coders first worked independently to recursively read the responses and develop coding schemas, and then later worked together to merge their codes and negotiate boundary items until the coding schema was valid and reliable. In addition to reporting numerical data, we also analyzed the data from the survey responses for statistical correlations by running Chi-square and ANOVA tests in JMP software. If a test shows a probability or p value of less than .05, it is considered statistically significant. As Isabelle Thompson et al. (2009) explain, "The p level indicates the extent to which the differences between the two groups would occur by chance" (p. 89). The statistically significant correlations in the data help to illustrate the mosaic of graduate student labor experiences.

Results and Discussion

We received 344 responses, including 215 PhD students, 74 MA/MS students, 19 MA/PhD students, and 36 MFA students. Students employed by at least 87 universities (not including four participants who did not list a university) reported on their experiences as GSIs. Across the 87 universities located in a total of 37 states, the majority of our survey participants were enrolled in public institutions (89.7%) with very high research activity levels (73.2%). Another 22% of GSIs serve in high research institutions, and the remaining 5% are in doctoral/professional universities and master's colleges and universities. In terms of our respondents' demographics, we had four open-ended questions that allowed GSIs to write in their gender, sexual orientation, race, and dis/ability. After coding these responses as described above, our overall respondents identify in the following ways. Gender identifications are 63% female, 27% male, 1% nonbinary or gender nonconforming, and 8% with no response. Sexual orientations are 53% heterosexual, 27% LGBQ, 2% asexual, >1% other, and 16% with no response. Dis/ability identifications are 15% disabled, 56% nondisabled, and 29% with no response. Racial identifications are 79.1% white, 4.9% Asian, 3.5% Hispanic or Latinx, 3.2% mixed race, 1.5% Black, and the rest no response—startling numbers we return to below.

Looking at the overall trends in the demographic data, the majority of respondents identified as white (79%), women (63%), nondisabled (56%), and heterosexual (53%). This data suggests that Strickland's observations on the imagined ideal writing teacher, a white woman, persist today. We believe that these overall trends support our claim that graduate programs imagine an idealized graduate student—white, nondisabled, and heterosexual with no dependents—which is problematic because graduate school is a pipeline to the professoriate. We point to both the quantitative data about GSI stipends, workload, and health benefits and their stories, gathered from our open-ended questions, to highlight how labor conditions construct an exclusive imagined ideal. Sections and subsections began with quotes from our respondents that speak to the overall themes.

Overworked and Underpaid: GSI Stipends & Workload

> "We deserve better pay and benefits for all the work we do. I love my job, but I'm not surviving financially, and I will no longer be continuing the program because of it."

We asked how many years GSIs received funding, the amount of funding, and its adequacy. Master's students typically receive two years of funding (~80%), MFA students are more often funded for three years (~68%), and doctoral students are typically funded for four (~40%) or five (~45%) years. A small number of GSIs (~5%) receive no funding whatsoever. On average, the 316 GSIs who responded to this survey question make $15,500 per year. The lowest yearly amount reported is $540, while the highest was $26,000. Table 1 presents average stipends alongside GSIs' perception of their funding.

Table 1

Average Stipends and Perception of Stipend Adequacy by Degree Programs

Program Level (n=344)	Average Stipend (n=316)	Stipend (In)Adequacy Yes = Adequate; No = Inadequate (n=341)	
MA/MS (n=74)	$11,184.50	No	55 (76%)
		Yes	17 (24%)
MA to PhD (n=19)	$16,786.90	No	13 (68%)
		Yes	6 (32%)
MFA (n=36)	$13,691.10	No	26 (72%)
		Yes	10 (28%)
PhD (n=215)	$16,607.70	No	150 (70%)
		Yes	64 (30%)

PhD students earn the highest stipends overall, to a degree that is highly statistically significant (<.0001). That instructors pursuing higher degrees earn higher stipends isn't shocking on its own (though the MFA degree is also terminal). What we find noteworthy is that GSIs across all ranks report their stipends are inadequate. Also, the dramatically lower pay for MA, MS, and MFA students leads us to question how the field of writing studies is considering—or more likely, not considering—the living needs and pedagogical value of masters-level and MFA GSIs.

Within programs, too, students report variation among pay with little transparency. As one respondent reported, "Pay rates are uneven for us. Some people have just negotiated for more money and it is given on an ad hoc basis. This is individual and not codified in any way, and, feels uneven." Such variation gives us concern. In our survey, across all demographic categories, white, cisgender male, nondisabled, and straight GSIs reported, on average, higher salaries than their nonwhite, women and nonbinary, disabled, and LGBT counterparts. We wonder if uneven GSI pay within departments might partially explain the pay inequity for various marginalized groups that we found in the data. Additionally, we did not ask about mandatory student fees, an oversight we regret as several respondents noted that their fees, not covered by tuition remission, eat up a large chunk of their stipend.

Stipend (In)adequacy

> "I think there is an overall assumption of economic privilege in my program, and many others. Our stipend is considered generous by administration in comparison with other programs, but it is still not much money at all and the only students satisfied seem to be the ones like me, who are young, have no dependents, no major expenses, able-bodied, from economic privilege, often white."

As we indicated in our research question, we were interested not only in the labor conditions of graduate writing programs, but also how students *experience* those conditions. As a result, we asked students if their stipend was adequate for covering their living needs (n=341). The overwhelming majority (71.6%) reported that their stipends were inadequate. When asked to describe how their stipends are adequate or not, 28 GSIs explained that their stipends do not or barely cover their cost of food. One respondent explains, "The English department here started a mini-food pantry for the GTAs affected and provided info for how to receive pay-advances so people could eat and make rent." Many others described sacrificing basic needs with complicated calculus. For instance, one GSI reports, "I have no room for emergencies. I can barely cover rent, utilities and groceries, but if, say, I get a flat tire, I've got to cut back on food so I can afford a new tire."

While 28.4% of respondents reported that their stipends were adequate, out of the 96 "adequate responses," approximately two-thirds offered important caveats to *why* their stipends were adequate. For instance, many GSIs who claimed their stipends were adequate explained that they have family or partner support, entered graduate school with no student debt, and/or do not have dependents. Others explained that their stipends may cover food and rent but aren't enough to cover medical emergencies or dental work. For instance, one respondent noted their stipend, "just barely covers living expenses; any emergencies/dr. appointments/extra needs send me into crisis mode." Low stipends, then, can prevent students from seeking out needed medical care. Another respondent claimed their stipend was adequate, but then elaborated, "Although I have to forgo some meals, I can usually get by each month." Therefore, we are comfortable insisting that while stipends may be adequate for some GSIs, that adequacy often requires sacrifice—such as medical care or meals. In other words, stipends are likely to be adequate for the imagined ideal GSIs: those with economic privilege and thus are more likely to be privileged along other axes of identity, e.g., white, single/childfree, cisgender, nondisabled.

Workload

> "I believe we should be given more money considering the amount of work we spend a week grading papers and preparing for class. I work about 30-35 hours a week, but am paid for 20 hours."

GSIs noted that their pay did not correspond with the amount of labor they contributed to the writing program. Or as one respondent more candidly phrased it, "too much work for too little pay." Indeed, 65.4% of GSIs overall reported working more hours than contracted, while just 26.8% reported working the same number of hours as contracted, and 7.5% reported working fewer than contracted. Table 2 demonstrates that the majority of GSIs report their contracted workload is 16-20 hours per week (68%), leading us to surmise that most programs feel that a GSI appointment should require this amount of work each week. The fact that only 25% of respondents reported working that number of hours, though, seems to suggest that writing program expectations do not align with GSI reality. This discrepancy suggests that programs (and perhaps students, too) may still frame the role of GSIs as apprenticeships, setting stipends at a fixed rate that does not align with workload.

Table 2

GSIs Reported Number of Hours Contracted to Work vs. Hours Actually Worked

Range of Hours	% of GSIs Contracted to Work Hours in that Range	% of GSIs Reported Hours Worked in that Range
Fewer than 10	N/A	1%
10-15	15%	12%
16-20	68%	25%
21-25	8%	20%
More than 25	3%	38%
Other	6%	2%

Even though the pay for the labor that they have been contracted to do fails to cover the living needs of 71.6% of GSIs, the majority of GSIs (65.4%) still do *more* work than they are actually contracted for. As for course load and credit hours, there is a clear disconnect between how many hours GSI employers *think* it takes to properly and ethically deliver quality instruction and how many hours GSIs feel obligated to work in order to do that work properly. As one respondent explains,

> We are required to teach two courses, with moderate guidance (given the syllabus and course assignments the week before that we should follow and have a meeting once a week) the first semester....*We work long hours to be the best teachers and this often comes at a sacrifice (health, sleep, our own studies).* (emphasis added)

Another survey respondent more bluntly articulated the links among stipends, workload, and student wellbeing, explaining, "A larger stipend would make it easier to justify how hungry I am despite how long I work." Our survey respondents speak to the tension between administrative expectations and GSI reality—and the impact of this tension on the health of GSIs. In order to meet the needs of their students, GSIs feel pressured to sacrifice their health, sleep, and studies, making it challenging to thrive as scholars, teachers, and humans.

Another factor that affects GSIs' perception of their stipend (in)adequacy is the number of hours they actually work, and as mentioned above, the majority of survey respondents (65.4%) are working more hours than their contract stipulates. Stipend adequacy and the number of hours that GSIs actually work are associated, as evidenced by a significant p value of 0.0110. Most GSIs (68%) are contracted to work 16-20 hours per week, but

38% of GSIs report working more than 25 hours per week. Therefore, it should be no surprise that the greatest number of GSIs who feel their stipends are inadequate work more than 25 hours per week (32%). In addition, there is a highly significant correlation between stipend amounts and stipend adequacy (p value of <.0001). As might be expected, GSIs reporting higher stipends tend to feel their stipends are more adequate than GSIs with lower stipends.

Taken together, these figures on stipend adequacy and workload strongly suggest that the standard compensation of GSIs assumes that GSIs are single and without dependents, have outside financial support, and require little to no medical care during their time as GSIs. Here, one GSI explains the prohibitive and exclusive nature of GSI stipends and high workload: "These assistantship programs are designed for healthy, young, single students. They are not appropriate for students with non-normative households, health issues or a lack of familial support." This observation echoes Bousquet's (2020) question about who is able to accept such poor labor conditions in the first place: "What does it mean that increasingly only persons who can 'afford to teach' are entering higher education as a profession?" (p. 98). It appears GSI packages are designed for an imagined ideal, scholar-teachers who aren't burdened by the need for food, childcare, or car maintenance. Given the wealth gap between white and non-white families in the United States, the expectation that GSIs will have outside support disproportionately threatens the success of GSIs of color—in particular, Black GSIs (de Souza Briggs, 2019). These assumptions, then, harm not only GSIs but also the field as a whole, as many underrepresented GSIs lack the material resources to thrive under the reported conditions. How can the field of writing studies strive for diversity in the professoriate if GSI compensation is designed for GSIs with economic privilege?

GSI Healthcare and Wellness

> "No dental insurance; no vision insurance; the copay is too high for therapy; the urgent care is too high; the deductible keeps increasing; no affordable option for birth control or other women's needs (I can't use my insurance [sic] for this; I go to an income-based facility in town)."

GSIs' experiences of stipends relate strongly to their experiences of healthcare benefits. The lower a GSI's stipend is, the less adequate they feel their healthcare and leave policies are. In the case of health care plans, there is a statistically significant correlation between reports of adequacy and the amounts of stipends (p value of <.0001). The correlation between the adequacy of leave policies and the amount of stipends is also statistically significant (p value of .0139). In other words, GSIs who are struggling to make ends meet with their stipends also face higher barriers in accessing healthcare—a critical component in GSI wellness and retention. Indeed, to get an overall picture of healthcare, we asked participants what kind of coverage is provided at their institutions, the cost of the plan(s), and ways the plan does or does not meet their needs. We also asked GSIs about their access to paid parental and medical leave in their programs. We unearthed sobering information about the state of health and wellness coverage, much of which can be characterized by lack of coverage, inadequacies in coverage, and GSIs' unfamiliarity with policies.

Lack of Healthcare Coverage

> "I don't have health insurance because I can't afford it on my own, and Florida doesn't offer medicaid for low-income indvidiuals [sic]."

We were happy to find that the majority of GSIs report having access to healthcare in some form. However, for far too many GSIs, the inadequate health coverage erects additional barriers in their pursuit of a graduate degree. Nearly 15% of respondents reported that no health care or stipend for coverage is offered by their program (see Table 3 for the full breakdown). In addition, many GSIs reported that their programs offered inconsistent or no coverage options for partners and children. For example, one respondent said, "My partner is also a graduate student at the same university. We each have a separate health care plan and we pay another company to insure our child, because our university health care plan does not cover spouses or children." Others reported that spousal coverage was either not available or too expensive.

Table 3

Types of Health Benefits (n = 343)

Types of Health Benefits	**% GSI Reported**
Student health insurance	57.7%
Student health insurance for GSI and dependent	35.6%
Employee health care plan (same as staff and faculty)	8.5%
Extra stipend to go toward health costs	5%
No health care or stipend offered	14.9%

For GSIs who are offered healthcare coverage, our survey respondents describe the variety of ways that the coverage is inadequate for their needs. Of the approximately 85% of GSIs who reported that their program did offer a healthcare plan, 40% (125 of 311 responses) indicated that their plan did not meet their healthcare needs. The most common reasons cited by participants were specific limitations of the health coverage offered (n=77) and the high cost of premiums, deductibles, and out-of-pocket expenses (n=70). One respondent explained, "The health plan is not guaranteed at the rate it currently is. I can't afford to stay here in the program if it is no longer subsidized." GSIs also reported that their plans did not cover certain types of care (e.g., dental, vision) and/or specific medications, procedures, and tests. For example, one respondent described their healthcare plan as adequate even as they reported their co-pays are often high and they do not have vision or dental coverage. Another GSI stated that dental coverage is not available and, "if I need to see a specialist, sometimes there are none in my area on my plan." Three respondents noted that their healthcare plan does not cover transgender healthcare services, creating an additional expensive barrier for trans GSIs. 11 respondents also explained that the available healthcare options do not cover dependents and/or spouses or the cost to cover dependents and/or spouses is prohibitive. Of those 11 responses, four claimed that dependent coverage was cut last year, a stark reminder of the liminality of GSIs: benefits can change in a moment's notice, creating abrupt crises for GSIs with health and/or caregiving needs. For GSIs who found their healthcare plans to be adequate, they stated that flexibility to choose healthcare providers, low premiums and copays, and the ability to cover partners and dependents were key to their satisfaction.

Inadequacies in Mental Health Coverage

> "I have generalized anxiety disorder, attention deficit disorder, and chronic depression. Our program has no infrastructure in place to help students and GAs with mental illness through the very difficult systemic hurdles starvation wages bring about."

In a separate question, we asked survey respondents whether their programs offer mental health and wellness support and (if applicable) how that support does or does not meet their needs. Responses indicated that 22% of GSIs are either not provided mental health and wellness support or are provided inadequate support. For example, 68 students reported limitations (e.g., to the number of appointments or selection of doctors) or high costs. One respondent shared that although their program does provide access to mental health services, "undergraduate and graduate students are only allowed to have 6 appointments at the Counseling Center total during their time at school. Afterward, we must find an off-campus therapist who takes our insurance." We highlight inadequacies in mental health support separately from health care plans partly because mental health support is a known concern for graduate students across disciplines (Evans et al., 2018; Grady et al., 2013; Perry, 2019). In their study of 2,279 graduate students from a variety of fields, Evans et al. (2018) found that "graduate students are more than six times likely to experience depression and anxiety as compared to the general population" (p. 282), highlighting the need for better access to mental health resources and additional training for faculty mentors.

Inadequacies in Parental and Medical Leave

> "As far as I know, we get unpaid leave, but the 'clock' keeps running. So a semester of leave is still part of the 5 years of funding we get (even though we didn't get funding for that semester)."

An even greater number of respondents said their program lacked parental and sick leave policies. Just 5.2% of respondents reported that their programs offer guaranteed paid parental leave, while 2.3% reported they had access to paid parental leave, but it was not guaranteed. Far more GSIs report that their program offers no official parental leave policy (37.6%). Similarly, 32.4% of respondents reported that their program offers no official medical leave policy. Of the GSIs who do have access to official medical leave, 12.8% report access to paid leave and 11.2% report access to unpaid leave.

Responses highlight the discrepancy between written leave policies and the cultural expectations of medical and parental leave practices. Several respondents explained that GSIs are instructed not to take leave at all (6.2%) or to arrange coverage of any missed classes due to sickness (2.8%). One respondent who was unaware of an official parental leave policy added, "My friend had a baby one semester and they let her register for one hour (so she could be continually enrolled), but she had to pay for it. They put her funding on hold and it started up again when she came back." Another respondent noted that though they did not know the leave policies of the program, they had observed graduate workers assigned online courses immediately following birth.

Finally, we also found that many respondents did not know the details of leave policies. Overwhelmingly, GSIs did not know their program's sick leave policies (31.2%) nor the parental leave policies of their program (37.6%). This data illustrates to us, then, that not only are GSIs often denied official leave policies in the face of birth, adoption, and/or sickness, but they also have to overcome pressure to return early and/or expend additional labor to find coverage for their missed classes. That so many GSIs lack knowledge of the official policies, too, points to an additional barrier if GSIs unexpectedly need to use parental or medical leave during their course of study.

Healthcare and Diversity

> "Having children is also a blessing, but personally it puts me at a disadvantage when it comes to my teaching preparation and research. There is little to no support to mitigate this, and our university yanked dependent coverage from us last year which put more of a strain on our finances and time."

GSIs enter graduate school with their whole bodies; they can't leave their health issues, disabilities, and/or family obligations at the door. What medical sacrifices, such as prescription medicine, vision and dental care, mental health support, are GSIs expected to make in order to pursue their graduate degrees? Ideally, none, and thus, we see the inadequacies of healthcare provided to GSIs to be a diversity issue. As one respondent notes, student health care plans are often designed for an imagined ideal young and healthy body: "I am over 50 years old, so the university health program is not designed for someone with my health needs, which includes leukemia monitoring and mental-health supports." The field of disability studies has long noted the increased barriers disabled and chronically ill scholar-teachers face in academia (Dolmage, 2017; Price, 2011). In addition to the stigma disabled and sick people may face in academia, a lack of comprehensive healthcare can prevent them from even entering the field. The imagined ideal of the healthy, nondisabled GSI leaves few options for sick and disabled GSIs: they must gain admission to one of the few programs that offer comprehensive and affordable healthcare, find alternative coverage, or leave programs.

Furthermore, limited healthcare options and leave programs threaten to exclude pregnant people, parents/caregivers, and future parents. By making dependent healthcare inaccessible through high cost or unavailability, universities threaten the financial and medical wellbeing of parent GSIs and their children. The parental leave policies reported can be similarly harmful, with many GSIs unsure of their options or pressured to not take leave at all. We find this especially troubling given the gender make-up of the respondents (63.37% identified as women). Of course, not all women can or want to have children, and men and non-binary people can have children. Still, women tend to take parental leave far more often than men for a variety of complicated medical, social, family, and financial reasons (Douglas-Gabriel, 2018).

Researchers, activists, and parents have long observed the benefits of parental leave programs for both children and parents, including a lower chance of postpartum depression (Kornfeind & Sipsma, 2018). When universities and academic programs limit parental leave, through lackluster policies, cultural pressure, or the absence of information on leave, they reinforce the archaic, yet persistently destructive myth, that academic parents—and particularly mothers—should either never allow their parenting selves to interfere with work or leave work completely (Hirakata & Daniluk, 2009; Tolentino, 2016). The inadequacies of health care and leave policies that our survey participants describe suggest that policies for GSI compensation are based on an imagined ideal GSI, and that graduate programs risk losing or not recruiting students who do not fit the imagined ideal in their programs.

Conclusion

Our findings reveal the overlooked, yet often dire, labor conditions of GSIs of writing. Indeed, many of the numbers and responses worry or even infuriate us, including the stories of GSIs devoting their time, energy, and care into teaching while struggling to pay rent or sacrificing meals and healthcare. As we hope our study has demonstrated, the labor conditions of GSIs reveal what we have called in this article the *imagined ideal*; it is this imagined ideal that preconditions GSIs to be exploited. In sum, the writing studies field has less than ideal labor conditions *because* it has grown accustomed to an unrealistic imagined ideal of GSIs.

We invite readers to imagine a new ideal with us, one that values the work of teaching writing, GSI labor, and the variety of bodies who contribute to this work. In this new ideal, we envision universities that pay GSIs a living wage, offer comprehensive and affordable healthcare to GSIs and their families, and provide clearly communicated medical and parental leave policies. To reimagine the mosaic of GSI labor conditions, we propose two critical re-framings that emerge from our data, re-framings that make room for more bodies and experiences in the profession.

Recognize GSI Labor as Labor

As we've articulated throughout this article, we insist on recognizing GSIs as workers—as students and mentees, of course, but also as workers deserving of food, shelter, and medicine. GSIs shouldn't have to choose between graduate study and healthcare, meals, and/or starting a family. If we value the knowledge-making of GSIs from diverse backgrounds in the writing classroom and the field, WPAs, faculty, and directors of graduate study must call for equitable labor conditions that allow GSIs to succeed as whole people. WPAs and graduate mentors might begin with the following seemingly small steps: solicit anonymous feedback from GSIs about their experiences of labor conditions in the program; provide measures for maintaining reasonable GSI workloads; increase transparency of graduate students' stipends at the institutional level; and clearly document and communicate health and medical care coverage, medical and parental leave policies, as well as procedures for accessing this coverage, during both recruitment and training phases of the graduate program. These steps might begin the significant work of recognizing GSI labor as labor and thus, create avenues for assessing and organizing around the material conditions of GSIs.

Attend to the Role of Labor Conditions in the State of Diversity of Our Field

In our conversations about the data, we kept returning to numbers on race in the demographics section: why so few respondents of color? We were not alone in expressing concern that almost 80% of respondents identified as white. Asao Inoue (2019) tweeted a screenshot of our initial report's demographic data with the note, "This is some of the demographic data from their report that should concern us all." The data does indeed concern us. We can look at these numbers in two ways: the first, that we failed in reaching out to GSIs of color in our outreach efforts, and the second, that the discrepancy reflects the racial make-up of our field. We believe that these possibilities are not mutually exclusive, but rather constitutive. Because our field is overwhelmingly white, labor research, advocacy, and practices often operate from a perspective of whiteness. In other words, the lack of diversity in our programs exacerbates the lack of diversity; when nondisabled, economically privileged, white, and/or single graduate students make up the majority of GSIs, discriminatory and inhumane labor conditions might remain invisible to faculty, administration, and researchers. Practically speaking, addressing this also means going beyond diversity and wellness programming and attending to the labor conditions of GSIs. Events promoting self-care for GSIs are great, for instance, but cannot replace affordable access to mental health care for GSIs of color. In other words, with better material conditions, we believe more students from diverse backgrounds will have a less arduous path to the professoriate.

Acknowledging Local Complexity, Proposing Heuristics

As we present these findings, we foresee two potential critiques: first, that our study largely avoids providing concrete solutions or examples of programs that have successfully addressed similar issues; and second, where it does so, it doesn't pay sufficient attention to the heterogeneity and local complexities of the writing programs within which GSIs work. This complexity of funding structures for GSIs; of WPA authority and positionality; of writing program architecture and ecology; of institutional history and procedures and more; makes us wary to provide monolithic solutions, or to suggest model programs. Nevertheless, we offer the following as some initial, heuristic steps for moving toward concrete action.

We encourage all WPAs and faculty—regardless of how they feel their programs stack up against this study—to critically analyze how their programs might create more equitable labor conditions regarding the following questions:

- How do contracts, policies, rules, and communication surrounding GSI labor assume an imagined ideal?
- What challenges might these pose for non-normative GSI bodies?
- What moves are within my power to support GSIs in easing or eradicating those challenges?

The first two questions are designed to spark reflection for the current state of GSI labor conditions—potentially *kairotic* to explore during discussions on recruitment, diversity, and retention—while the final question pushes us to think creatively about how we might support minoritized GSIs. For instance, how might WPAs compensate Black, Indigenous, and GSIs of color for the diversity work that is often thrust upon them in writing programs? How might teaching workloads be adjusted to account for the increased care work of GSIs with young children during a pandemic? To put it crudely, we are calling for a praxis of knowing when to break shit, when to fix shit, and when to subvert shit. This praxis requires stakeholders in GSI advocacy to reflect on their local contexts and take *kairotic* action in solidarity.

WPAs, GSIs, and non-GSI writing faculty cannot transform labor conditions on their own. Indeed, in our observations, WPAs have largely assumed labor advocacy as a huge part of their role, and now that many of the authors of this article have transitioned into faculty and lecturer roles, we intend to do the same. For us, writing programs are one starting point for large-scale mobilization on behalf of GSIs, a generative home for the grad worker organization movements already brewing across the U.S.

Furthermore, as we continue our advocacy work, the field of writing studies can consider how other systems of oppression—white supremacy, sexism, classism, ableism, homophobia, transphobia, colonialism—intersect with the experiences of GSIs in writing programs. Schell (2017) reminds us that labor "organizing strategies can break down if questions of white privilege and bodily difference are not addressed" (xvi). By keeping Schell's calls in mind, we can foreground the lived experiences of the most vulnerable GSI bodies in writing programs. In doing so, GSI organizers, WPAs, and writing faculty at all ranks can align our field's expressed values—diversity, equity, representation—with our daily practices, allowing GSIs from all backgrounds to thrive as teachers, scholars, and human beings.

Acknowledgments

This project would have not been possible without the tireless, unpaid labor of our fellow taskforce members, who were all also GSIs while they contributed to the study: Katie McWain, Julianna Edmonds, Jacki Fiscus-Cannaday, Leah Heilig, Laura Matravers, Stacy Rice, and Hillary Yeager.

Notes

1. Data were collected in accordance with IRB Protocol #17-275 at Virginia Tech.

References

Barnum, M. (2016, August 22). Why teacher pay matters: Recruitment and retention can improve results. *The 74*. https://www.the74million.org/article/why-teacher-pay-matters-recruitment-and-retention-can-improve-results/

Bérubé, M. (2013, February 18). The humanities, unraveled. *The Chronicle of Higher Education*. https://www.chronicle.com/article/Humanities-Unraveled/137291

Bousquet, M. (2002). The waste product of graduate education: Toward a dictatorship of the flexible. *Social Text, 20*(1), 81-104.

Colaneri, L. (2019, August 29). Five myths and one truth about graduate worker unions. *Strikewave*. https://www.thestrikewave.com/original-content/2019/8/28/five-myths-and-one-truth-about-graduate-worker-unions

Cole, K. (2019). No body is disinterested: The discursive materiality of composition in the university. In A. Alden, K. Gerdes, J. Holiday, and R. Skinnell (Eds.), *Reinventing (with) theory in rhetoric and writing studies* (pp. 149-166). Utah State University Press.

Creswell, J. W. (2014). *Research design: Qualitative, quantitative and mixed methods approaches* (4th ed.). SAGE Publications, Inc.

Crowley, S. (1998). *Composition in the university: Historical and polemical essays*. University of Pittsburgh Press. https://muse.jhu.edu/book/27049

de Souza Briggs, X. (2019, July 8). The racial wealth gap: A stark reflection of structural inequality. Ford Foundation. https://www.fordfoundation.org/ideas/equals-change-blog/posts/the-racial-wealth-gap-a-stark-reflection-of-structural-inequality-lessons-learned-from-two-decades-of-work/

Dolmage, J. T. (2017). *Academic ableism: Disability and higher education*. University of Michigan Press.

Douglas-Gabriel, D. (2018, May 1). Harvard agrees to negotiate a contract with graduate-student union. *The Washington Post*. https://www.washingtonpost.com/news/graduatee-point/wp/2018/05/01/harvard-agrees-to-negotiate-a-contract-with-graduate-student-union/?noredirect=on

Elder, C. L., Schoen, M., & Skinnell, R. (2014). Strengthening graduate student preparation for WPA work. *WPA: Writing Program Administration 37*(2). 13-35.

Evans, T. M., Bira, L., Gastelum, J. B., Weiss, L. T., & Vanderford, N. L. (2018). Evidence for a mental health crisis in graduate education. *Nature Biotechnology*, *36*, 282–284. https://doi.org/10.1038/nbt.4089

Grady, R. K., La Touche, R., Oslawski-Lopez, J., Powers, A., & Simacek, K. (2014). Betwixt and between: The social position and stress experiences of graduate students. *Teaching Sociology*, *42*(1), 5–16. https://doi.org/10.1177/0092055X13502182

Griffin, J. A., Keller, D., Pandey, I., Pedersen, A. M., & Skinner, C. (2005). Local practices, institutional positions: Results from the 2003-2004 WCRP national survey of writing centers. *Writing Centers Research Project*.

Hirakata, P., & Daniluk, J. C. (2009). Swimming upstream: The experience of academic mothers of young children. *Canadian Journal of Counselling*, *43*(4), 283–294. https://pdfs.semanticscholar.org/c2ee/ef7635678548be588e-3a680cfe1252f09da8.pdf

Inoue, A. B. (2019, March 21). And this is some of the demographic data from their report that should concern us all. [Tweet]. https://twitter.com/AsaoBInoue/status/1108900619803189248

Kahn, S., Lalicker, W. B., & Lynch-Biniek, A. (Eds.) (2017). *Contingency, exploitation, and solidarity: Labor and action in English composition*. WAC Clearinghouse and University Press of Colorado.

Kesslen, B. (2019, June 8). The latest campus battle: Graduate students are fighting to unionize. *NBC News*. https://www.nbcnews.com/news/us-news/latest-campus-battle-graduate-students-are-fighting-unionize-n1015141

Kornfeind, K. R., & Sipsma, H. L. (2018). Exploring the link between maternity leave and postpartum depression. *Women's Health Issues: Official Publication of the Jacobs Institute of Women's Health*, *28*(4), 321–326. https://doi.org/10.1016/j.whi.2018.03.008

Liggett, S., Jordan, K., & Price, S. (2011). Mapping knowledge-making in writing center research: A taxonomy of methodologies. *Writing Center Journal*, *31*(2), 50–88.

MLA Survey of Departmental Staffing. (2014). Modern Language Association.https://www.mla.org/Resources/Research/Surveys-Reports-and-Other-Documents/Staffing-Salaries-and-Other-Professional-Issues/Data-from-the-MLA-Survey-of-Departmental-Staffing-Fall-2014

Mountford, R. (2002). From labor to middle management: Graduate students in writing program administration. *Rhetoric Review, 21*(1), 41–53.

Perry, D. M. (n.d.). How to make graduate school more humane. *Grist*. https://psmag.com/ideas/graduate-school-continues-to-ignore-students-with-disabilities

Price, M. (2011). *Mad at school: Rhetorics of mental disability and academic life*. University of Michigan Press.

Samuels, R. (2017). *The politics of writing studies: Reinventing our universities from below*. University Press of Colorado.

Schell, E. (2017). Foreword. In Kahn, S., Lalicker, W. B., & Lynch-Biniek, A. (Eds.), *Contingency, exploitation, and solidarity: Labor and action in English composition*. WAC Clearinghouse and University Press of Colorado.

Strickland, D. (2011). *The managerial unconscious in the history of composition studies*. Southern Illinois University Press.

Thompson, I., Whyte, A., Shannon, D., Muse, A., Miller, K., Chappell, M., & Whigham, A. (2009). Examining our lore: A survey of students' and tutors' satisfaction with writing center conferences. *The Writing Center Journal, 29*(1), 78–105.

Tolentino, J. (2016, February 12). Fathers and childless women in academia are 3x more likely to get tenure than women with kids. *Jezebel*. https://jezebel.com/fathers-and-childless-women-in-academia-are-3x-more-lik-1758704068

Watlington, C. (2019, June 6). The labor movement's newest warriors: Graduate students. *The New Republic*. https://newrepublic.com/article/154097/labor-movements-newest-warriors-graduate-students

Wright, A.L. (2017). The rhetoric of excellence and the erasure of graduate labor. In S. Kahn, W.B. Lalicker, and A. Lynch-Biniek (Eds.), *Contingency, exploitation, and solidarity: Labor and action in English composition* (pp. 271-278). The WAC Clearinghouse; University Press of Colorado. https://doi.org/10.37514/PER-B.2017.0858 https://wac.colostate.edu/books/perspectives/contingency/

Ruth Osorio is Assistant Professor of Rhetoric and Women's Studies at Old Dominion University.

Allison Hutchison is Senior Lecturer in the Engineering Communications Program at Cornell University.

Sarah Primeau is Associate Director of the First-Year Writing Program at University of Illinois at Chicago.

Molly E. Ubbesen is Assistant Professor of Writing at University of Minnesota Rochester.

Alexander Champoux-Crowley is a PhD candidate in the Rhetoric, Scientific and Technical Communication program at University of Minnesota Twin Cities and lecturer at University of Southern Maine.

Book Review

Emotional Identity and Dexterity: A Review of *The Things We Carry*

Jackie Hoermann-Elliott

Adams Wooten, Courtney, Jacob Babb, Kristi Murray Costello, and Kate Navickas, editors. *The Things We Carry: Strategies for Recognizing and Negotiating Emotional Labor in Writing Program Administration*. Utah State UP, 2020. 350 pages.

Last winter break, I found a long-awaited sense of shelter in the pages of *The Things We Carry: Strategies for Recognizing and Negotiating Emotional Labor in Writing Program Administration.* In the academic year prior, I lost a close friend and colleague, subsequently assumed a new WPA role, gave birth to my second child a month later, and then responded to the pandemic's switch to emergency remote teaching and learning. Needing respite from the storms of work and life, my intention was to read *The Things We Carry* to feel less alone, to connect with other WPAs whom I knew I would not be seeing at our annual conference any time soon. On top of this desire for connection and support, I picked up this book hoping to find peer-reviewed validation for the daily emotional labor I have never had the courage to list as a legitimate bullet point in my periodic performance review materials. What I found was more than calming assurance and professional affirmation to hang my hat on. Across all fifteen chapters and corresponding strategy sheets, this well-curated collection expands overlooked and sometimes suppressed aspects of the WPA's identity. With the sociological lens of emotional labor as a guiding light and other related theoretical lenses illuminating new paths forward, *The Things We Carry* takes us on a tour of the WPA emotional dimensionality—the parts we share, the parts we hide, and the parts that some of us, especially jWPAs, don't know well enough yet.

Beginning with a timely reflection on the impacts of both the COVID-19 pandemic and the Black Lives Matter protests, the preface draws on the collective goal of the twenty-three featured authors as being one that is needed now more than ever. Adams Wooten, Babb, Costello, and Navickas position more recent events in connection to the larger theoretical conversations about emotional labor that are well underway in other fields of study, but that WPA scholarship has been slow (or perhaps too emotionally inundated) to unpack. With these new hardships come opportunities to question existing systems in thoughtful ways. In the Introduction, Costello and Babb recount MSNBC news anchor Rachel Maddow's very public emotional breakdown in reporting on the internment of infants and children in juvenile detention centers in South Texas. They unpack why Maddow's visible display of emotions shocked viewers (and even Maddow herself) and how this televised moment provides an interesting point of comparison for when we, as WPAs, feel dispossessed of our right to display raw, unadulterated emotion.

In three distinct sections, the emotional dexterity of the WPA is plotted out in terms of identity at work, within larger community networks, and more intimately within themself. The first five chapters nested into section one revolve around the preservation of work identities, "examin[ing] the emotional labor of different WPA contexts and discourses and offer[ing] strategies for making that emotional labor more visible and productive" (11). Perhaps somewhat of a tongue-in-cheek title, "Don't Worry, Be Happy: How to Flourish as a WPA" by Carrie S. Leverenz is the first chapter in this section and one sincerely endeavoring toward helping WPAs use positive psychology to strengthen positive feelings that often take a backseat to negative feelings and realities associated with administrative work. With personal narrative and interdisciplinary research, she sets the stage for us to understand why we as academics are so overly critical of ourselves, and with all of Leverenz's signature frankness in tone, she concludes by telling us that in order to find happiness we "have to work at it" (35). For me, this first chapter was particularly meaningful, as I see myself in these pages, quite literally, having been one of the three pregnant graduate instructors who caused Leverenz additional stress in her first semester returning to WPA work. Now in my role as Director of an FYC program, I have graduate teaching assistants confiding in me about their family planning timelines and asking how they can harmoniously balance having a new baby with their 2/2 teaching loads and dissertation writing schedules—a conversation rife with opportunity for more scholarly conversation and support.

The next two chapters offer perspectives that are unique to specific institutions and positions woven with strands of wisdom that any WPA can appreciate. In "You Lost Me at 'Administrator': Vulnerability and Transformation in WPA Work at the Two-Year College," Anthony Warnke, Kirsten Higgins, Marcie Sims, and Ian Sherman unveil the relentless demands community college faculty face when heavier teaching loads come to bear on their scholarly and activist-oriented endeavors. And yet, Warnke et al. reveal an internal challenge specific to two-year college WPAs, whose faculty colleagues can resist the official ordination of a writing program for fear of losing their instructional autonomy. No simple solution will absolve two-year college faculty, those who are or who aspire to be WPAs, of this burden, but these authors suggest that "The essential truth of a WPA affecting positive change in a two-year college writing program is that we have to learn to work effectively and gracefully both with and against the emotions evoked by change in our colleagues and ourselves" (Warnke et al. 46). In chapter 3, "The Emotional Labor of Becoming: Lessons from the Exiting Writing Center Director," Kate Navickas presents a method grounded in her own experiences entering a new position for determining the negative, the positive, and the unknowns WPAs may face: conducting "emotional labor interviews" with the writing center director (WCD), or other administrator, who precede us (56). Not only do these interviews provide an opportunity to gauge the institutionally specific emotional demands of one's inherited position, but they help create a clearer picture of how our own preconceived notions of disciplinary identity come to bear on our new realities as teacher-scholar-administrators. Navickas explains, "There is emotional labor around the identity of the WCD when the job doesn't align with disciplinary narratives of work and one's sense of what it should involve" (68). For administrators in non-tenure-line or staff positions, her words will ring true and offer possibilities for reimagining our emotional work within our new roles.

Like many WPAs who were trained to play (and write) by the rules, I was forced by the last two chapters in section one to ask unexpected questions of myself as a scholar and an administrator. In "Educating the Faculty Writer to 'Dance with Resistance': Rethinking Faculty Development as Institutional Transformation," Janelle Adsit and Sue Doe critique Kerry Ann Rockquemore, a beloved authority on faculty writing support who founded the National Center for Faculty Development and Diversity (NCFDD), for her programming that operates based on a deficit pedagogy model. Rockquemore, they contend, more or less blames faculty for not finding enough time to write; instead, Adsit and Doe cite the increasingly unsustainable workloads placed on faculty and administrators, who are asked to teach and publish more than is reasonable. Adsit and Doe write that when we "internalize the metrics of productivity forwarded by groups like the NCFDD," we merely reify the "rhetorics of success" that hold us down (77).

In the book's next chapter, Amy Ferdinand Stolley analyzes survey research from 51 WPAs who self-identified as having engaged in emotional labor over their careers. I was stunned that as many as 70% of these participants discussed their emotional labor in professional documents as a way of teaching colleagues about the affective knowledge they employ to serve both students and faculty (103). For those seeking a chapter that verifies and values WPA emotional work in promotion and tenure discussions, Stolley's contribution provides data to normalize this practice as well as strategies for self-inventorying individual circumstances.

I could relate to Kim Hensley Owens' chapter on "Handling Sexual Assault Reports as a WPA" because the crises of 2020 also brought a sharp rise in the number of Title IX cases reported by students enrolled in writing classes at my university. Owens situates readers within her heart-wrenching account of one fall semester in which she dealt with an appalling number of campus sexual assault cases, one occurring between two students enrolled in an FYC course. Her assessment of what unfolded and how she responded returns the focus to how emotional labor involves "surface acting" or what "people do when trying to convey one emotional state while feeling another [that] typically results in increased fatigue" (Owens 122). Her activist response—providing more sexual assault prevention resources—boosted awareness among her FYC teachers, who were better able to support students experiencing this type of trauma. Likewise, Kaitlin Clinnin's chapter unpacking her response to the 2017 Las Vegas Strip shootings makes a compelling argument for seeing WPAs as "programmatic crisis responders," on top of their growing list of invisible responsibilities. Clinnin provides a framework for processing what WPAs need to do beyond merely responding to immediate concerns, offering a model of "prevention, preparedness, response, and recovery process of crisis response" that's useful for new crises (Clinnin 134). Relatedly, chapter 8 by Carl Schlachte takes us through his experiences as an adjunct instructor at CUNY Brooklyn, where his contingent faculty status left him feeling unsure how to handle his classes when Hurricane Sandy made landfall. He advises WPAs on how to foster a program culture in which instructors of all ranks feel a sense of agency and confidence during disasters, rounding out a three-chapter stretch exploring trauma-informed care as it pertains to administrative work.

Later in the second section, Matthew T. Nelson, Sam Deges, and Kathleen F. Weaver demonstrate how "significant emotional work is required for everyone working in a writing center," including tutors (162). With evidence from psychology, they show that tutors who started tutoring sessions feeling stressed remained stressed or experienced an increased level of stress while tutoring (166). They also provide some ideas for alleviating the stress and anxiety many tutors report, which is desperately needed given how little WPA scholarship has addressed the emotional weight these all-important associates have long shouldered. Finishing this section, Elizabeth Imafuji's chapter uncovers how she, as a solitary WPA, handled a student confession of pregnancy at her religiously affiliated institution, where premarital sex violates a strict code of student conduct. This chapter, frequently cross-referenced by other chapters for good reason, helps readers consider how Kim Hensley Owens' practical actions can carry forward into moments when students need help navigating university bureaucracy; sometimes moments of surface acting find happy endings.

The final section begins with two of the arguably most kairotic chapters in the collection, given the urgency of efforts to increase diversity and equity. First, Sheila Carter-Tod's "Administrating While Black: Negotiating the Emotional Labor of an African American Female WPA." In the last five years or so, Carter-Tod and other Black WPAs have written about the marginalization they face as WPAs of color (Phelps et al. 15). She presents survey and interview research to unearth the micro- and macro-aggressions Black WPAs face at programmatic, departmental, and university levels. Carter-Tod points out that a simple list of strategies won't bring about necessary systemic change; all WPAs need to "promote inclusion as a way of negotiating emotional labor by creating and supporting initiatives that draw future and current Black female WPAs into a pipeline of support through recruitment and mentoring" (Carter-Tod 212). In chapter 12, conversations about WPAs' intersectional identities continue with Joseph Janangelo candidly sharing the workplace shaming he endured for years and the survival tactics that helped his career, albeit not necessarily his emotional well-being. Using multiple theoretical and even popular culture perspectives, he poses deeply contemplative questions pertaining to bullying, and he reminds us that "anger can be transformative" (Janangelo 225).

In "From Great to Good Enough: Recalibrating Expectations as WPA," Elizabeth Kleinfield takes us unexpectedly into her public and private grieving process after the loss of one of the peer tutors she worked closely with in her writing center. Death is a difficult topic in any context, but it is especially challenging to process in smaller programmatic circumstances in which, whether comfortably acknowledging or not, a sense of family or friendship has formed. No WPA scholar I have encountered has written guidelines for how to deal with and publicly respond to the death of a tutor, teacher, or administrator in a program—understandably so, considering what a difficult and easily criticized undertaking that could become. Nevertheless, Kleinfield, gives gentle guidance for administrators who are grieving or, inevitably, have grieved. In chapter 14, Christy I. Wenger extends her contemplative writing pedagogical expertise to the role of the WPA, taking self-care from being just another buzzword and arguing for "a relational understanding of emotional labor approached through mindfulness, one that keeps the WPA in focus but also understands her emotions ecologically as sources of agency, actionable tools, and not only a means of control or workplace oppression" (Wenger 256). Courtney Adams Wooten's "How to Be a Bad WPA" Wooten asks us to consider which "happiness scripts" help or hurt us, and she defines cruel optimism so that we might better understand what could divest us of our emotional bandwidth. She leaves us with a question as her parting thought: "What would happen if more of us—or all of us—decided to be bad WPAs *and to tell others about it*?" (Adams Wooten 282).

The concluding chapter positions us to trace back through the vulnerable, unfiltered truths these scholars have shared so that, going forward, WPAs will be better positioned to recognize emotional squall lines that threaten to wreak havoc on our lives at and outside of work. *The Things We Carry* does not leave the reader with injunctions for growth but no resources, of course. Strategy sheets that accompany the book's chapters recapture key phrases, concepts, and recommendations so that readers can identify solutions in a pinch. These sheets suggest that the editors and the contributors who came together in these pages imagined a text that was more than a deeply intellectual contribution. *The Things We Carry* aims to be accessible to administrators at any point in their career, whether needing quick support or finding themselves feeling too overloaded or too emotionally drained. The book positions itself to be an authority on emotional labor in WPA circles; however, I suspect this work will encourage many more scholars to keep the conversation going for years to come.

Works Cited

Carter-Tod, Sheila. "Reflecting, Expanding, and Challenging: A Bibliographic Exploration of Race, Gender, Ability, Language Diversity, and Sexual Orientation and Writing Program Administration." *WPA: Writing Program Administration*, vol. 42, no. 3, 2019, pp. 97–105.

Phelps, Louise Wetherbee, Sheila Carter-Tod, Jessie L. Moore, Patti Poblete, Casey Reid, and Sarah Elizabeth Snyder. "Sustainable Becomings: Women's Career Trajectories in Writing Program Administration." *WPA: Writing Program Administration*, vol. 43, no. 1, 2019, pp. 12–32.

Jackie Hoermann-Elliott is Director of First-Year Composition and Assistant Professor of English at Texas Woman's University, where she teaches courses on and studies the role of the body in the writing process. Her book, *Running, Thinking, Writing: Embodied Cognition in Composition,* was released this year (Parlor Press, 2021).

Review Essay

Compassion and Social Justice: What We Can Learn from *Sixteen Teachers Teaching*

Charles Grimm

Sixteen Teachers Teaching: Two-Year College Perspectives, edited by Patrick Sullivan. Utah State UP, 2020. 309 pages.

Cheri Lemieux Spiegel, Darin Jensen, and Sarah Z. Johnson's Summer 2020 issue of *WPA* focused on WPA work in the two-year college (2YC), providing insights from WPAs in various 2YCs, where WPA positions rarely exist with clearly defined positions and boundaries. Patrick Sullivan's recent collection of essays, *16 Teachers Teaching*, offers further insight into the 2YC world and its peculiarities of staffing, teaching, and learning. Authors in this volume range from adjuncts to established professors to student authors, whose voices too frequently do not appear in scholarly literature. This inclusive cross-section of the 2YC forwards one primary purpose: pedagogy as democratic action.

In his introduction, Sullivan introduces social action as inherent in teaching in the 2YC, recounting its origin in the 1947 Truman Commission, which sought to create more leaders for a nation desperately wanting leadership. In 2019, 34% of students enrolled in post-secondary education were enrolled in two-year colleges, marking a high degree of success for Truman's plan ("Undergraduate Enrollment"). Sullivan divides his collection into five parts: An Introduction to Teaching Writing at the Two-Year College, Teaching Informed by Compassion and Theory, Equity and Social Justice at the Two-Year College, New Approaches to Teaching Developmental Reading and Writing, and a Conclusion. From advocacy programs to food pantries, from adjuncts publishing from their position of precarity to theoretically-informed graduate students finding themselves unfamiliar with how to teach actual students, *16 Teachers Teaching* contains voices that seek an audience with writing program administrators.

In keeping with the democratic ethos of 2YCs that keeps student voices at the forefront, this review recognizes the insights students offer before discussing the chapters written by instructors. Bridgette Stepule opens the student chapters, emphasizing flexibility for students in the 2YC who desire education amid busy lives of family, work, and other concerns that remove a four-year degree from their immediate futures. Stepule specifies that teachers who kept their focus on what students needed rather than on formatting and mechanics provided her the greatest benefit. Lydia Sekscenski adds encouragement as a key to successful 2YC instruction, reminding instructors that constructive feedback and positive reinforcement that encourages students to believe in themselves are heard above harsh criticisms in lives already steeped in hardship.

In the second section of the collection, Darlene Pierpont recounts her own struggles through English courses. The familiar discomfort of learning through reading and the fear of making grammatical errors pepper her account of this time, but in these classes she benefitted from teachers who were passionate about their subjects, who were patient in their approach to student writing, and who showed compassion to students. Similarly, Kevin Rodriguez defines the boundary of useful instruction: "teachers who were both organized and engaging (found ways to connect with the students) created the most enjoyable, thoughtful, and memorable learning experiences for me" (129). He warns that humor alone can open students up but also cause some students not to take the course seriously, and he adds that asking about students' lives without following up detracts from students' perception that professors care.

The third section includes Lauren Sills' view that 2YCs' lack of the gatekeeping mechanisms of standardized test scores and high school GPAs allow 2YCs to exist as a true community with the respect and natural diversity often lacking in larger institutions. In the fourth section, Jamil Shakoor similarly locates Real Life within his education. He acknowledges the hard work required for students entering mostly in developmental programs and appreciates the way the professors keep responding to drafts with a mixture of understanding and intellectual rigor. Remediation, a term he introduces into his text, prepared Shakoor for success to such a degree that he argues strongly that any attempt to remove remedial courses from students who did not grow up with the privilege of strong schools and/or family structures "is founded on a serious lack of *real-life* experience" (246, italics original). Thus Sills and Shakoor leave the reader with narratives of what community looks like, with first-hand accounts from the students 2YCs serve describing their desire to be met where they are in their educational journeys. For students, then, a successful writing program depends more on engaging students meaningfully rather than on the theoretical approaches or assessments the field of writing program administration may find more comfortable.

Turning from the student-authored to professionally-authored chapters, disparity becomes a recurring theme for 2YC contexts, often most notably in how to treat struggling people as people rather than problems. Perhaps it is fitting, then, that Darin Jensen's chapter opens the first section with an unflinching description of the world of the contingent writing teacher in the 2YC. Acknowledging the precarity of his own position along with the precision of his professional work makes teaching that much harder, because teaching about democratic principles while being excluded from those same principles serves to underscore the "tension of two competing realities and ideologies" (42). Similarly, Sullivan's interview of Helene Adams Androne points out the friction between instructors' demands in teaching, scholarship, and service, encouraging readers to link the three in as many teaching tasks as possible to build momentum in all three areas with a focus on helping students. She concludes "What [our students] do and how they find success matters to many more around and behind them, so facilitating their journeys is a privilege. We must keep learning and working hard for their sakes and for the future of all of our communities" (64). In closing Part 1 of the book, Sullivan provides the reader with a cross section of life at the two-year college, touching briefly on many of the victories as well as the continuing struggles, priming the reader for the compassion requested in Part 2.

Brett Griffiths opens Part 2 of *16 Teachers Teaching* by describing a visit to her school's writing center as a student, where she was met by a calmer voice than she had found in instructor feedback on her papers. Now, as the director of a writing center, she encourages teachers to meet students "who they are" (74). This means asking genuine questions about the welfare of the writer and responding helpfully, even walking students to various campus resources that help meet their material needs. The literacy sponsorship Griffiths describes allows students to find opportunities to re-situate themselves as writers and appreciate mistakes as opportunities to learn, while Klausman describes a course that provides direction through transfer. As a WPA, he set up reading groups to discuss multiple texts concerning how to help students take knowledge from writing classes forward. Designing his course for transfer required "the explicit teaching of key terms, the essential role of reflection, and the development of theory" (93) within a framework that allows primary research, some structured writing, and consistent returns to reflections. By the end of the semester, his students create their own theory of what college writing is or should be so that they can adopt this model in other courses as they continue their education. Just as Griffiths actively encourages compassion, Klausman actively encourages clear application that meets students' needs beyond English classrooms, both of which embody what Jeffrey Andelora explains as the need for TYC faculty to be researchers.

Sullivan's interview with Jeffrey Andelora runs the gamut from discussing treating students with respect to designing a course to engaging with scholarship. Throughout the interview, Andelora balances the need for instructors to be active in their research on the front lines of composition teaching as well as being present with the students they have in their classes. Most notable, however, is Andelora's realization: "I noticed the lack of two-year college voices in the field of composition, and was struck by the fact that the theorists, the knowledge-makers, were those who for the most part didn't teach much composition, yet two-year college faculty were teaching five sections of it every semester. Where was our voice?" (122). Andelora praises those who have taken the time to commit to research on top of heavy teaching and/or administration loads, but he states that the type of drive and enjoyment people get from research should not differ greatly from the enjoyment of reading and writing that led many of us to become English teachers in the first place (123). Regardless of whether instructors publish, Andelora leaves readers with the final exhortation: "figure out how to stay fresh, how to bring something new to the classroom. We owe that to our students. … find a practice that will sustain you over the long haul. The richness you bring to the classroom is only as deep as your enthusiasm for being there" (124). For this particular 2YC instructor, these words weigh heavily – Andelora's break-up speech at the 2018 CCCC that announced the beginning of the TYCA national conferences gave me just such a boost when losing my way as a graduate student despairing of finding an academic job. Since then, TYCA has been sustaining for me.

Holly Hassel opens the third section, which focuses on equity and social justice, by discussing critical information literacy as a necessary skill in first-year composition. Hassel details how working in writing centers, moonlighting at community colleges, and taking writing theory and pedagogy courses while a grad student did not prepare her for the classroom. Her preliminary approach worked poorly for those not yet acclimated to academia, causing a mutual frustration between teacher and students. It was not until she discovered the scholarship of teaching and learning that she was able to fit all the pieces of assessment, placement, and development into a meaningful arrangement for the students in her classes at community colleges. Regarding the possibility of frustration, Hope Parisi reminds readers that each student in every class in the 2YC context has overcome struggles to be in that seat (155). Parisi asks teachers to view low performance as a chance to intervene in an area of a student's life where they may be facing scarcity rather than to make meritocratic assumptions about the student's worth. This choice, Parisi argues, advances social justice by focusing on who we have in the classroom rather than who we wish we had.

Hassel and Parisi both advocate using multiple low-stakes assignments with ample feedback to meet students where they are and to serve as sign posts for students trying to re-enter a course later in the semester. Rather than defeat students, Hassel and Parisi structure their courses to celebrate student accomplishment.

Of particular significance at this point in the CWPA's continued pursuit of social justice and equity, the final chapter of the social justice section comprises an examination of a single institution's ongoing struggle to achieve racial equity among instructors at both the departmental and institutional level. The saga details some faculty members' work to incorporate critical race theory into job descriptions, inquests to expose racism against candidates and/or colleagues, and the reticence of the institution to engage in frank discussions of the role of race in hiring and maintaining its workforce. Discussions at their institution broke down quickly into tone policing, silence, or underground conversations, rendering the heartbreaking summary "We broke. We are still broken" (180). Even as these authors found a publisher interested in publishing their account of antiracist labor, they encountered a lack of willingness to market the book, even at the largest disciplinary conferences where their presentation was being awarded. The authors of this chapter ask the question all institutions concerned with social justice must ask: from individual teachers to whole institutions, how can we rise up against perpetuating historical injustices? Their eight bulleted answers offer practical and necessary solutions for our current rhetorical situation that explain the significance of silence and the complexity of historical colonization and subjugation, but their conclusion holds the hope for how to fix what is broken: "we need these texts, and the decolonizing practices within them, to get into the hands of writing teachers across the country, one teacher at a time if necessary" (198).

The fourth major section deals with basic writing (BW) in the 2YC context. Gallagher argues that teaching BW provides a necessary component of learning for professors. Due to the wide variation in writing and reading skills, each class becomes a custom-made course to help students learn to improve their writing. Gallagher draws attention to the ways antiracist pedagogy can help students engage in this progress by including a "Language and the Politics of Proper English Essay Prompt" along with a consideration of how allowing students to use their vernacular language in an academic essay better prepares students to evaluate their language choices. Giordano picks up this same concept, extending it further to encourage BW content that challenges students while showing them in manageable stages what college-level work looks like. These courses, just as Gallagher argued, need to be individually tailored to the students taking them, not as an additional burden to overloaded teachers but as a means of directing ownership of readings and writing assignments to students. In an effort to help teachers or programs tasked with building dynamic BW programs, Giordano also includes multiple resources for assignments, schedules, and evaluations. Peter Adams completes the section on BW with a critical reflection on his 10 years of experience with the ALP, including a generous packet of materials, but he explains in greater length than the other authors the difficulty of teaching BW just after completing a graduate program. Few graduate students get direct experience with or instruction in BW due to institutional initiatives to remove BW courses paired with a sustained focus in many graduate programs to emphasize that securing a job at an R1 school is the only acceptable job market outcome.

Leah McNeir helps conclude the collection with a chapter written to new English teachers. McNeir encourages teachers to remember what makes them passionate about the work of teaching so that they can keep that focus during challenging times. She also encourages new teachers to remember that they have a duty to their students to help students take ownership of their education, which touches back on the impetus for the creation of community colleges detailed in the book's introduction. The final chapter contains Sullivan's interview with Howard Tinberg, a celebrated figure in TYC communities as an author, editor, and chair of national organizations. Perhaps the most intriguing question Sullivan poses is why someone would choose to teach at a 2YC rather than settle for teaching at one. Tinberg answers by providing insight into his own initial ignorance concerning the work at a 2YC before explaining the richness in diversity at 2YCs that represents the surrounding community, and the willingness of students at a 2YC to work hard, encapsulating attitudes within the classroom and in many students' lives outside of the classroom. Tinberg's closing words offer a vision of FYC as a space that creates better citizens, a vision that fits our cultural moment for teachers and students as it offers true hope.

Many of the chapters in this collection demonstrate the close connection of two-year college scholars to the classroom, and many chapters speak to the lack of sufficient graduate-level training in community college and basic writing programs. These two issues go hand-in-hand: as a recent graduate teaching assistant who left his assistantship at an R1 to take on a full-time position at a 2YC, I learned directly and indirectly that research matters more than teaching to many people in academia. In speaking glowingly of this book, I practice the same praise I do for my students outside the classroom: many people already look down on the work, so I will stand to advocate for its sincerity and intensity. *Sixteen Teachers Teaching* offers a critique that WPAs and those training future WPAs in graduate programs need to pay attention to and account for within the field by offering coursework and professional development opportunities specifically focusing on BW and 2YC contexts, and not just FYC "in general," a term which often defaults to representation of SLACs and universities.

As noted in the review above, this book also offers a way to think through the CWPA's current situation regarding anti-racist labor. It offers solidarity for those who have spoken up, especially those who have been censured in various ways. It offers background for those who have not yet investigated the implications of critical race theory for institutions. And, in the way that literature often does, it provides an external account that all sides of the CWPA reckoning with white supremacy can approach as an external rather than personal event to weigh arguments more fairly. I believe any fair reading of Coleman, DeLong, DeVore, Gibney, and Kuhne's chapter will promote acceptance of the solutions that they offer for individuals, as the conclusion calls for, or for institutions willing to do that difficult work.

Works Cited

"Undergraduate Enrollment." *National Center for Education Statistics*, May 2021, nces.ed.gov/programs/coe/indicator/cha. Accessed 31 May 2021.

WPA: Writing Program Administration, edited by Cheri Lemieux Spiegel, Darin Jensen, and Sarah Z. Johnson, vol. 43, no. 3, summer 2020.

Charles C. Grimm is Assistant Professor at Georgia Highlands College, a rural community college northwest of Atlanta, where he teaches composition. He is currently ABD at Georgia State University with a dissertation investigating the usefulness of ghostwriting as both a corporate and educational practice, with an expected spring 2022 defense date.

Extending an invitation to join the

Council of

Writing Program Administrators

The Council of Writing Program Administrators offers a national network of scholarship and support for leaders of college and university writing programs.

Membership benefits include the following:

- A subscription to *WPA: Writing Program Administration*, a semi-annual refereed journal
- Unrestricted access to journal archives and job boards
- Participation on WPA committees and task forces
- Invitations to the annual WPA Summer Workshops and Conferences
- Invitations to submit papers for sessions that WPA sponsors at MLA and CCCC
- Participation in the WPA Research Grant Program, which distributes several awards, ranging from $1,000 to $2,000
- Invitation to the annual WPA breakfast at CCCC
- Information about the WPA Consultant-Evaluator Service

Membership Rates

- Lifetime Membership GOLD: print journal, conference registration, and membership for life: $3,000
- Lifetime Membership SILVER: print journal and membership for life: $1,500
- Member Level 3 (income over $100,000): $150/year (Green option: $125*)
- Member Level 2 (income $40,000-$100,000): $100/year (Green option: $80*)
- Member Level 1 (income under $40,000): $55/year (Green option: $45*)
- Student Member: $30/year (Green option: $20*)
- Emeritus Member: $30/year (Green option: $20*)
- Institutional Membership (1 print journal to institution and 1 WPA membership, including journal): $250

*Green option - receives digital journal in lieu of print journal

For More Information

Visit us online at http://wpacouncil.org.

PARLOR PRESS
EQUIPMENT FOR LIVING

Now with Parlor Press!

Studies in Rhetorics and Feminism
Series Editors: Cheryl Glenn and Shirley Wilson Logan

New Releases

Writing Spaces: Readings on Writing Volume 4

Running, Thinking, Writing: Embodied Cognition in Composition
by Jackie Hoermann-Elliott

English Studies Online: Programs, Practices, Possibilities, edited by William P. Banks and Susan Spangler

Feminist Circulations: Rhetorical Explorations across Space and Time, edited by Jessica Enoch, Danielle Griffin and Karen Nelson

Pedagogical Perspectives on Cognition and Writing, edited by J. Michael Rifenburg, Patricia Portanova, and Duane Roen

MLA Mina Shaughnessy Prize and CCCC Best Book Award 2021!

Creole Composition: Academic Writing and Rhetoric in the Anglophone Caribbean, edited by Vivette Milson-Whyte, Raymond Oenbring, and Brianne Jaquette

Check Out Our New Website!

Discounts, blog, open access titles, instant downloads, and more.

www.parlorpress.com

WPA Discount: Use WPA20 at checkout to receive a 20% discount on all titles not on sale through November 1, 2021.

www.ingramcontent.com/pod-product-compliance
Lightning Source LLC
Chambersburg PA
CBHW031321160426
43196CB00007B/611